Cooking Light
chicken
tonight!

Cooking Light

chicken
tonight!

Oxmoor House®

ISBN-13: 978-0-8487-3322-3
ISBN-10: 0-8487-3322-3
Library of Congress Control Number: 2009937184

Printed in the United States of America
First Printing 2010

Be sure to check with your health-care provider before making any changes in your diet.

Oxmoor House, Inc.

VP, Publishing Director: Jim Childs
Editorial Director: Susan Payne Dobbs
Brand Manager: Terri Laschober Robertson
Managing Editor: Laurie S. Herr

Cooking Light Chicken Tonight!

Senior Editor: Heather Averett
Project Editor: Diane Rose
Senior Designer: Emily Albright Parrish
Director, Test Kitchens: Elizabeth Tyler Austin
Assistant Director, Test Kitchens: Julie Christopher
Test Kitchens Professionals: Allison E. Cox, Julie Gunter, Kathleen Royal Phillips, Catherine Crowell Steele, Ashley T. Strickland
Photography Director: Jim Bathie
Senior Photo Stylist: Kay E. Clarke
Associate Photo Stylist: Katherine Eckert Coyne
Production Manager: Theresa Beste-Farley

Contributors

Compositor: Carol Damsky
Copy Editor: Jacqueline B. Giovanelli
Proofreader: Julie Gillis
Indexer: Mary Ann Laurens
Interns: Georgia Dodge, Perri K. Hubbard, Allison Sperando, Christine Taylor

Cooking Light

Editor: Scott Mowbray
Creative Director: Carla Frank
Deputy Editor: Phillip Rhodes
Food Editor: Ann Taylor Pittman
Special Publications Editor: Mary Simpson Creel, M.S., R.D.
Nutrition Editor: Kathy Kitchens Downie, R.D.
Associate Food Editors: Timothy Q. Cebula, Julianna Grimes
Associate Editors: Cindy Hatcher, Brandy Rushing
Test Kitchen Director: Vanessa T. Pruett
Assistant Test Kitchen Director: Tiffany Vickers Davis
Senior Food Stylist: Kellie Gerber Kelley
Recipe Testers and Developers: SaBrina Bone, Deb Wise
Art Director: Fernande Bondarenko
Deputy Art Director: J. Shay McNamee
Junior Deputy Art Director: Alexander Spacher
Photo Director: Kristen Schaefer
Senior Photographer: Randy Mayor
Senior Photo Stylist: Cindy Barr
Photo Stylist: Leigh Ann Ross
Copy Chief: Maria Parker Hopkins
Assistant Copy Chief: Susan Roberts
Research Editor: Michelle Gibson Daniels
Editorial Production Director: Liz Rhoades
Production Editor: Hazel R. Eddins
Art/Production Assistant: Josh Rutledge
Administrative Coordinator: Carol D. Johnson
Cookinglight.com Editor: Allison Long Lowery

To order additional publications, call 1–800–765–6400 or 1-800-491-0551.

For more books to enrich your life, visit **oxmoorhouse.com**

To search, savor, and share thousands of recipes, visit **myrecipes.com**

Cover: Chicken Scaloppine with Broccoli Rabe, page 113
Back cover (clockwise from top left): Cilantro-Lime Chicken with Avocado Salsa, page 125; Tex-Mex Chicken Tortilla Soup, page 239; Spiced Chicken Kebabs, page 87; Hot Chicken and Chips Retro, page 22; Chicken with 40 Cloves of Garlic, page 137; Biscuit-Topped Chicken Potpie, page 148

introduction

As a busy home cook, you want one thing: simple, quick, healthy dishes to serve your family on hectic weeknights. And if you're like most cooks, chicken more than likely holds the place as the most reliable staple of many of your meals. But can chicken really win rave reviews around your dinner table several nights a week? How do you keep it interesting—and flavorful? The answer—*Cooking Light Chicken Tonight!*

Because your family wants more than the same old "healthy" chicken recipes, we—the editors of *Cooking Light* magazine—have pulled from our arsenal of the very best chicken recipes for this comprehensive collection of quick and easy chicken dishes. With over 150 recipes and photos, this book is guaranteed to expand your weeknight-cooking repertoire.

And since you don't need just another collection of recipes, we've also pulled out all the stops to create a chicken cooking guide. The **Cooking Class** (page 8) offers all the basics for preparing chicken—from purchasing and safely handling chicken to sautéing chicken breasts and creating pan sauces.

With *Cooking Light Chicken Tonight!,* our dedicated staff of culinary professionals and registered dietitians gives you all the tools and recipes you'll need to prepare healthful, delicious chicken dishes any night of the week. From family-pleasing **Pan-Fried Chicken** (page 133) and **Spicy Honey-Brushed Chicken Thighs** (page 167) to good-enough-for-company **Chicken Potpie** (page 151) and **Roasted Chicken with Onions, Potatoes, and Gravy** (page 174), these kitchen-tested recipes breathe new life into the idea of having *Chicken Tonight!*

The *Cooking Light* Editors

contents

cooking class

Chicken is a perennial favorite among *Cooking Light* readers—and with good reason. It is versatile, straightforward, and in our recipes, always delicious. With this Cooking Class highlighting all the ins and outs of cooking chicken, you'll be ready for chicken tonight!

Chicken Safety

Chicken is highly perishable and should be handled carefully to prevent food-borne illness. Check the "sell by" date on the package label before purchasing. This shows the last day the product should be sold.

Storing: Refrigerate raw chicken for up to two days and cooked chicken for up to three days. Raw skinless, boneless chicken can marinate in the refrigerator for up to 8 hours; raw chicken pieces with skin and bone can marinate for up to one day. Freeze uncooked chicken up to six months and cooked chicken up to three months.

Thawing: You can thaw frozen chicken in the refrigerator or in cold water. Allow about five hours per pound of frozen chicken to thaw in the refrigerator. For the cold-water method, submerge the chicken—still in its wrapping—in a sink or pot of cold water, and change the water every 30 minutes until it's thawed.

Handling: Wash your hands well with hot water and plenty of soap before and after handling raw chicken. Use hot water and soap to wash the cutting board and any utensils that come in contact with the chicken. When you rinse chicken, be careful that you don't splash water from it onto countertops where unwrapped foods such as fruit, vegetables, or salad greens may be.

Cooking: To prevent food-borne illnesses, chicken must be cooked to 165°. For whole birds, use an instant-read thermometer inserted in the thickest part of the thigh to confirm the temperature. For breasts, legs, and thighs, pierce with the tip of a knife—when it's done, the flesh should be opaque, and the juices should run clear.

Chicken Glossary

Here's our guide to commonly purchased chicken.

Broiler-fryers: Broiler-fryers are about seven weeks old, and they weigh 3 to 4 pounds. They're good for making stock (they're not as meaty as roasters) and will work in any recipe that calls for a cut-up fryer.

Roasters: At three to five months old, roasters weigh 4 to 7 pounds. If you want to bake a whole chicken, look for a roaster—they have the highest meat-to-bone ratio.

Stewing hens: At 10 months to 1½ years old, stewing hens are literally tough old birds. They're best used for chicken and dumplings or soup; when roasted, they're almost jaw-exhausting.

Cornish game hen: The term Cornish game hen is a misnomer. These small birds are actually a cross between Cornish game roosters and White Rock hens; despite the gender-specific name, both male and female birds are sold. At a month old, they weigh about 1½ to 2 pounds. Roasting works best for these petite birds.

Boneless, skinless chicken breasts: We often use this cut in our Test Kitchens because chicken breasts are lean and versatile. You can buy them with the skin on, but be sure to remove the skin before eating it—you can easily remove the skin and fat with kitchen shears.

Chicken thighs: Either bone-in or skinless, chicken thighs are higher in fat than breasts, but they have a succulent and hearty flavor and a firmer flesh that work well in dishes with a longer cook time.

Chicken roaster

Dark meat is higher in fat and generally works better in recipes that cook slowly.

The white meat, with the skin removed, contains the leanest meat.

Purchasing Info

When purchasing chicken there are many options. Let the ingredients list for the recipe be your guide.

Fresh whole chicken (broiler-fryers, roasters, and stewing hens): For more information on whole chickens see the chicken glossary on page 10.

Organic and free-range chicken: Organic and free-range chickens have a "cleaner" chicken flavor and a better texture than conventionally farmed chicken. The thing you need to consider is whether you believe they are worth the extra expense. Unless you're cooking simple roasted chicken, probably not.

Fresh chicken pieces (breasts, tenders, and thighs): Fresh chicken comes packaged in many ways. Read the labels carefully to check for specific pieces, size and weight, and for added flavor enhancers.

Frozen chicken: Individually frozen portions of bone-in and boneless breast halves, tenders, thighs, and drumsticks are readily available. They are frozen individually and packed loosely in resealable bags. Remove what you need for a given recipe, and keep the remainder frozen.

Precooked chicken: If your recipe calls for cooked chicken and you don't have any leftovers to use, you have options: poached chicken breasts, refrigerated or frozen cooked chicken, or store-cooked chicken. The store-cooked chicken (also known as deli-roasted or rotisserie chicken) is our favorite option. A rotisserie chicken keeps for three to four days in the refrigerator and is great to keep on hand for a quick meal.

Rotisserie chicken

Cooking Techniques

Sautéing

Chicken breasts are a staple of healthful cooking because they're lean and cook in a flash. Cook chicken breasts, deglaze the caramelized juice and browned bits in the pan with liquid, add a few other seasonings, and you're ready for supper in less than 30 minutes. For the best results, use a nonstick skillet, and scrape up the sauce thoroughly from the bottom of the pan to get the concentrated flavor left behind by sautéing.

How to sauté skinless, boneless chicken breasts and make pan sauce:

1. Trim away the fat and any small pieces of meat.
2. Place the breast between plastic wrap. Pound to a ½-inch thickness so it cooks quickly and evenly.
3. To tell if the chicken is done, pierce it with a fork. If the juices run clear, it's done.
4. After adding liquid to the pan, scrape the bottom to loosen the browned bits. This will add flavor to the sauce.
5. Pour the sauce into a measuring cup to be sure that it has reduced enough.

Consider your sautéed chicken a blank canvas. All you need to dress it up are pan and no-cook sauces. Here are six high-flavor options.

White Wine Sauce: Heat a skillet over medium-high heat. Coat pan with cooking spray. Add ⅓ cup finely chopped onion to pan; sauté 2 minutes, stirring frequently. Stir in ½ cup fat-free, less-sodium chicken broth, ¼ cup dry white wine, and 2 tablespoons white wine vinegar; bring to a boil. Cook until reduced to ¼ cup (about 5 minutes). Remove from heat; stir in 2 tablespoons butter and 2 teaspoons finely chopped fresh chives. Yield: 6 tablespoons (serving size: 1½ tablespoons).

CALORIES 59; FAT 5.7g (sat 3.6g, mono 1.5g, poly 0.2g); PROTEIN 0.6g; CARB 1.6g; FIBER 0.4g; CHOL 15mg; IRON 0.2mg; SODIUM 90mg; CALC 8mg

Spicy Orange Sauce: Heat a skillet over medium-high heat; coat with cooking spray. Add 1 tablespoon grated ginger; sauté 1 minute, stirring constantly. Stir in ⅔ cup fat-free, less-sodium chicken broth, 3 tablespoons orange marmalade, and 1½ tablespoons low-sodium soy sauce; bring to a boil. Cook until mixture is slightly thick. Stir in 1½ teaspoons fresh lemon juice and ¾ teaspoon sambal oelek (or other hot chile sauce). Yield: about ¾ cup (serving size: about 3 tablespoons).

CALORIES 45; FAT 0.1g (sat 0g, mono 0.1g, poly 0g); PROTEIN 0.8g; CARB 11.2g; FIBER 0.4g; CHOL 0mg; IRON 0.2mg; SODIUM 273mg; CALC 10mg

Tangy Mustard Sauce: Heat 2 teaspoons olive oil in a skillet over medium-high heat. Add 2 minced garlic cloves to pan; sauté 30 seconds, stirring constantly. Stir in ¼ cup dry white wine, ¼ cup fat-free, less-sodium chicken broth, 2 tablespoons maple syrup, and 2 tablespoons Dijon mustard; bring to a boil. Cook until reduced to ¼ cup (about 5 minutes), stirring occasionally.

Stir in ¾ teaspoon chopped fresh rosemary and ½ teaspoon freshly ground black pepper. Yield: ¼ cup (serving size: 1 tablespoon).

CALORIES 54; FAT 2.3g (sat 0.3g, mono 1.7g, poly 0.3g); PROTEIN 0.3g; CARB 8.2g; FIBER 0.2g; CHOL 0mg; IRON 0.3mg; SODIUM 87mg; CALC 13mg

Parsley Pesto: Place 2 cups fresh flat-leaf parsley leaves, 2 tablespoons toasted pine nuts, 1½ tablespoons grated fresh Parmigiano-Reggiano cheese, 1 teaspoon extra-virgin olive oil, and ¼ teaspoon salt in a food processor; process until smooth. Yield: ½ cup (serving size: 2 tablespoons).

CALORIES 59; FAT 4.8g (sat 0.7g, mono 1.9g, poly 1.6g); PROTEIN 2.3g; CARB 2.8g; FIBER 1.2g; CHOL 2mg; IRON 2.1mg; SODIUM 211mg; CALC 64mg

Creamy White Sauce: Combine ¼ cup canola mayonnaise, 2 teaspoons white vinegar, 1 teaspoon fresh lemon juice, ½ teaspoon freshly ground black pepper, ¼ teaspoon salt, and 1 minced garlic clove, stirring well. Yield: about ⅓ cup (serving size: about 4 teaspoons).

CALORIES 47; FAT 4.5g (sat 0g, mono 2.5g, poly 1.5g); PROTEIN 0.1g; CARB 0.5g; FIBER 0.1g; CHOL 0mg; IRON 0mg; SODIUM 238mg; CALC 2.4mg

Classic Vinaigrette: Combine 1½ tablespoons red wine vinegar, 1 tablespoon chopped shallots, ¼ teaspoon salt, 1 tablespoon Dijon mustard, and ⅛ teaspoon pepper. Gradually add 3 tablespoons extra-virgin olive oil, stirring until incorporated. Yield: 6 tablespoons (serving size: 1½ tablespoons).

CALORIES 94; FAT 10.1g (sat 1.4g, mono 7.4g, poly 1.1g); PROTEIN 0.1g; CARB 0.7g; FIBER 0g; CHOL 0mg; IRON 0.1mg; SODIUM 178mg; CALC 2mg

Pan-Frying and Oven-Frying

Pan-frying entails cooking food in a moderate amount of fat in an uncovered pan. It's similar to sautéing but requires more fat and often lower temperatures. Oven-frying utilizes the oven to mimic deep-frying by breading foods and then baking using a moderate amount of oil. The coating of flour and breadcrumbs helps create the desired crisp crust and also insulates the chicken breast to prevent it from overcooking.

How to bread a chicken breast

1. Pound chicken breast between 2 sheets of heavy-duty plastic wrap.

2. Working with 1 chicken breast at a time, dredge breast in flour, turning to coat. Shake off excess flour.

3. Dip floured chicken breast in egg mixture.

4. Dredge chicken breast in breadcrumb mixture.

Braising

Long, slow cooking is essential to success with this technique. This process marries the flavors, and the moist heat tenderizes inexpensive cuts of meat.

How to braise chicken

1. Use a large deep skillet so the heat is diffused and food cooks evenly. The diameter of the base should be about three times the height of the sides. If it's too shallow, moisture will evaporate easily, and the food can dry out as it cooks. Check periodically, and if the liquid dips too far down, top it off. Start with large pieces of meat. Here we're using bone-in chicken pieces because they take longer to cook than boneless. Brown the meat in the skillet.

2. Begin to build flavor in the dish by adding vegetables, spices, and herbs. Add hearty ingredients like tough root vegetables, spices, and dried herbs to the skillet early, and allow them to cook and flavor the dish. It's best to garnish with delicate chopped fresh herbs just before serving.

3. Create a bouquet garni by wrapping ingredients such as sprigs of fresh herbs, peppercorns, or bay leaves in cheesecloth. Place the bundle in the skillet to infuse the cooking liquid and meat as the dish simmers.

4. To achieve the best results, partially submerge the meat in a flavorful liquid as it cooks. Broth, milk, cream, cider, beer, wine, or spirits are all good options. Plain water is also useful in casseroles.

Roasting

Few entrées are as familiar and welcoming as a succulent roast chicken. It can be the star of both homey weeknight suppers and company-worthy dinners. Roast chicken's broad appeal is well deserved because its neutral-tasting meat harmonizes with many flavors.

How to roast chicken & make gravy

1. Separate the skin from the meat, and rub the seasoning mixture directly on the meat.

2. Tie the legs of the chicken together with kitchen twine for a professional presentation.

3. The bird cooks more evenly when it's elevated off the pan atop vegetables or a rack.

4. Insert the thermometer into the meaty part of the thigh to get an accurate temperature reading. This is the slowest-cooking part of the bird.

5. For a substantial fat savings, remove and discard the skin before serving.

6. Use a sharp knife to remove the legs first.

7. Hold the knife parallel to the chicken breast, and slice thinly.

8. Combine the pan drippings with a liquid, such as broth or wine, and drain off the fat.

9. Place the roasting pan over medium-high heat, and pour the liquid (along with the remaining drippings) back into the pan, scraping to loosen all the delicious browned bits. Add a bit of flour and a little more liquid, and cook until thick.

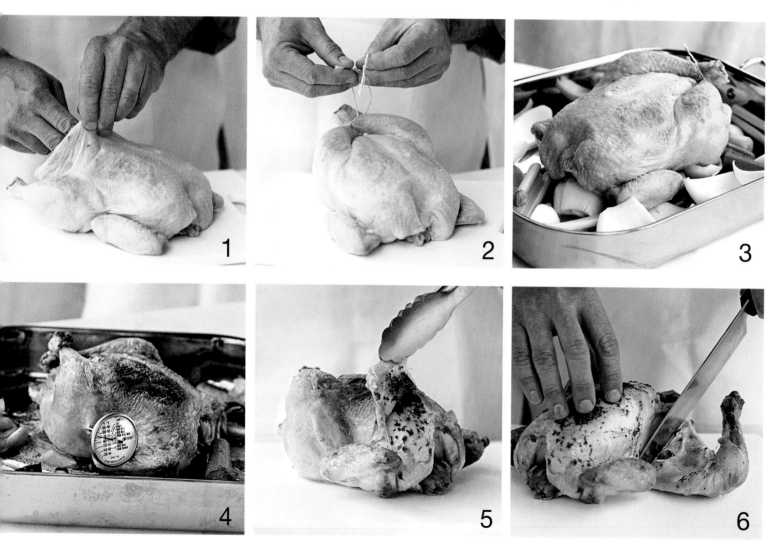

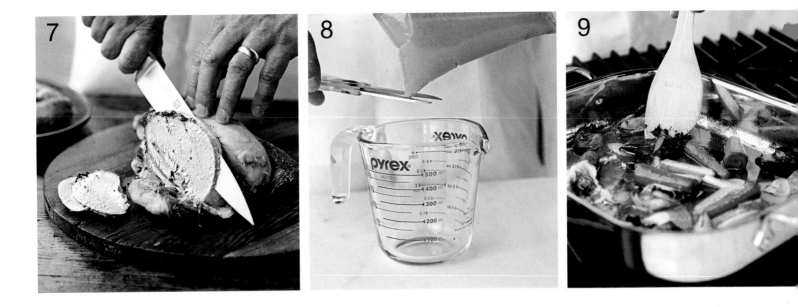

Grilling

Grilling chicken is an easy way to transform this humble food. You'll get the best results if you let the chicken stand out at room temperature before grilling.

How to grill chicken

1. Prepare the grill for indirect grilling with one hot side and one side without a direct source of heat.

2. If you plan to baste with a glaze as the chicken cooks, remove the skin before cooking; this allows the flesh to absorb the flavor of the glaze and brown nicely at the same time. (Chicken that is not glazed should be grilled with the skin on to shield the meat and keep it moist.)

3. Brown the chicken over direct heat. Then cook it over indirect heat, brushing it with glaze (if using) each time it's turned. Be sure to let the chicken stand 10 minutes before serving.

one-dish
meals

Chicken Tetrazzini

Chicken Tetrazzini combines cooked vermicelli, chicken, and mushrooms with a rich sherry–Parmesan cheese sauce. The mixture is sprinkled with breadcrumbs and Parmesan cheese and baked until bubbly and golden. This is a great way to use leftover cooked chicken.

Yield: 2 casseroles, 6 servings each (serving size: about 1⅓ cups)

1 tablespoon butter

Cooking spray

1 cup finely chopped onion

⅔ cup finely chopped celery

1 teaspoon freshly ground black pepper

¾ teaspoon salt

3 (8-ounce) packages presliced mushrooms

½ cup dry sherry

3 ounces all-purpose flour (about ⅔ cup)

3 (14-ounce) cans fat-free, less-sodium chicken broth

2¼ cups (9 ounces) grated fresh Parmesan cheese, divided

½ cup (4 ounces) block-style ⅓-less-fat cream cheese

7 cups hot cooked vermicelli (about 1 pound uncooked pasta)

4 cups chopped cooked chicken breast (about 1½ pounds)

1 (1-ounce) slice white bread

1. Preheat oven to 350°.

2. Melt butter in a large stockpot coated with cooking spray over medium-high heat. Add onion, celery, pepper, salt, and mushrooms, and sauté 4 minutes or until mushrooms are tender. Add sherry; cook 1 minute.

3. Lightly spoon flour into a measuring cup; level with a knife. Gradually add flour to pan; cook 3 minutes, stirring constantly with a whisk (mixture will be thick). Gradually add broth, stirring constantly. Bring to a boil. Reduce heat; simmer 5 minutes, stirring frequently. Remove from heat.

4. Add 1¾ cups Parmesan cheese and cream cheese, stirring with a whisk until cream cheese melts. Add pasta and chicken, and stir until blended. Divide pasta mixture between 2 (8-inch-square) baking dishes coated with cooking spray.

5. Place bread in a food processor, and pulse 10 times or until coarse crumbs form. Combine breadcrumbs and remaining ½ cup Parmesan cheese, and sprinkle evenly over pasta mixture.

6. Bake at 350° for 30 minutes or until lightly browned. Remove from oven; let stand 15 minutes.

CALORIES 380; FAT 12.2g (sat 6.6g, mono 3.4g, poly 0.7g); PROTEIN 33g; CARB 32.7g; FIBER 2g; CHOL 66mg; IRON 2.8mg; SODIUM 964mg; CALC 319mg

FLAVOR TIP

Parmesan is full of flavor, so a little goes a long way. Buy the real thing, which has Parmigiano-Reggiano printed on the rind. It has a sharper taste and a firmer texture than domestic Parmesan.

Hot Chicken and Chips Retro

This recipe has a nostalgic appeal that harks back to the 1950s and '60s. If you make it ahead, don't add the potato chips until it's time to bake the casserole, or they'll become soggy.

Yield: 6 servings

4 cups chopped roasted skinless, boneless chicken breast (about 4 breasts)

¼ cup chopped green onions

¼ cup chopped red bell pepper

2 tablespoons finely chopped fresh flat-leaf parsley

1 (8-ounce) can sliced water chestnuts, drained and chopped

½ cup low-fat mayonnaise

¼ cup reduced-fat sour cream

2 tablespoons fresh lemon juice

2 teaspoons Dijon mustard

½ teaspoon salt

½ teaspoon freshly ground black pepper

Cooking spray

¾ cup (3 ounces) shredded Swiss cheese

¾ cup crushed baked potato chips (about 2 ounces)

1. Preheat oven to 400°.
2. Combine chicken and next 4 ingredients in a large bowl; stir well. Combine low-fat mayonnaise and next 5 ingredients in a small bowl, stirring with a whisk. Add mayonnaise mixture to chicken mixture; stir well to combine. Spoon chicken mixture into an 11 x 7–inch baking dish coated with cooking spray, and sprinkle with cheese. Top cheese evenly with chips. Bake at 400° for 13 minutes or until filling is bubbly and chips are golden.

CALORIES 321; FAT 10.9g (sat 4.1g, mono 2.6g, poly 1g); PROTEIN 34.3g; CARB 20.4g; FIBER 2.6g; CHOL 96mg; IRON 11.4mg; SODIUM 606mg; CALC 175mg

QUICK TIP

To crush baked potato chips for the casserole topping, place the chips in a large zip-top plastic bag. With a meat mallet or rolling

pin, crush the chips by lightly pounding or rolling until you achieve the desired size and texture. This method makes clean-up a breeze and keeps crumbs in the bag.

Chicken and Broccoli Casserole

For crispier broccoli, remove it from the boiling water after three minutes.
Serve with a simple green salad.

Yield: 8 servings (serving size: about 1 cup)

3 quarts water

1 (12-ounce) package broccoli florets

4 (6-ounce) skinless, boneless chicken breast halves

1 ounce all-purpose flour (about ¼ cup)

1 (12-ounce) can evaporated fat-free milk

¼ teaspoon salt

¼ teaspoon freshly ground black pepper

Dash of nutmeg

1 cup fat-free mayonnaise

½ cup fat-free sour cream

¼ cup dry sherry

1 teaspoon Worcestershire sauce

1 (10.75-ounce) can condensed 30% reduced-sodium 98% fat-free cream of mushroom soup (such as Campbell's), undiluted

1 cup (4 ounces) grated fresh Parmesan cheese, divided

Cooking spray

1. Preheat oven to 400°.

2. Bring water to a boil in a large Dutch oven over medium-high heat. Add broccoli, and cook 5 minutes or until crisp-tender. Transfer broccoli to a large bowl with a slotted spoon. Add chicken to boiling water; reduce heat, and simmer 15 minutes or until done. Transfer chicken to a cutting board; cool slightly. Cut chicken into bite-sized pieces, and add chicken to bowl with broccoli.

3. Lightly spoon flour into a dry measuring cup; level with a knife. Combine flour, evaporated milk, salt, pepper, and nutmeg in a saucepan, stirring with a whisk until smooth. Bring to a boil over medium-high heat; cook 1 minute, stirring constantly. Remove from heat. Add mayonnaise, next 4 ingredients, and ½ cup cheese, stirring until well combined. Add mayonnaise mixture to broccoli mixture; stir gently until combined.

4. Spoon mixture into a 13 x 9–inch baking dish coated with cooking spray. Sprinkle with remaining ½ cup cheese. Bake at 400° for 50 minutes or until mixture bubbles at edges and cheese begins to brown. Remove from oven; let cool on a wire rack 5 minutes.

CALORIES 276; FAT 7.8g (sat 3.5g, mono 1.8g, poly 1.1g); PROTEIN 31.1g; CARB 18.9g; FIBER 2.1g; CHOL 66mg; IRON 1.6mg; SODIUM 696mg; CALC 365mg

Green Chile–Chicken Casserole

Just about every New Mexican home has a favorite version of this recipe. In the old days, canned soup was not available, but now cooks have the convenience of canned cream of chicken soup. Leftover turkey works in this recipe, too.

Yield: 12 servings (serving size: about ¾ cup)

1⅓ cups fat-free, less-sodium chicken broth

1 cup canned chopped green chiles, drained

1 cup chopped onion

1 cup fat-free sour cream

¾ teaspoon salt

½ teaspoon ground cumin

½ teaspoon freshly ground black pepper

2 (10½-ounce) cans condensed 98% fat-free cream of chicken soup (such as Campbell's), undiluted

1 garlic clove, minced

Cooking spray

24 (6-inch) corn tortillas

4 cups shredded cooked chicken breast (about 1 pound)

2 cups (8 ounces) finely shredded sharp cheddar cheese

1. Preheat oven to 350°.

2. Combine first 9 ingredients in a large saucepan, stirring with a whisk. Bring to a boil, stirring constantly. Remove from heat.

3. Spread 1 cup soup mixture in a 13 x 9–inch baking dish coated with cooking spray. Arrange 6 tortillas over soup mixture, and top with 1 cup chicken and ½ cup cheese. Repeat layers, ending with cheese. Spread remaining soup mixture over cheese. Bake at 350° for 30 minutes or until bubbly.

CALORIES 335; FAT 10.8g (sat 5.9g, mono 2.7g, poly 1.2g); PROTEIN 23.9g; CARB 34.3g; FIBER 3.2g; CHOL 66mg; IRON 1.5mg; SODIUM 693mg; CALC 270mg

MAKE-AHEAD TIP

If you assemble the casserole the day before, cover with cooking spray–coated foil and refrigerate. When ready to serve the dish, bake 1 hour; then uncover and bake an additional 30 minutes or until the cheese is bubbly and browning.

Chicken Chilaquiles

For even more heat, add ¼ teaspoon ground red pepper to the tomatillo mixture. You can have this from kitchen to table in 45 minutes. Serve with coleslaw and fruit on the side.

Yield: 4 servings (serving size: 1½ cups)

2 cups shredded cooked chicken breast

½ cup chopped green onions

½ cup (2 ounces) shredded Monterey Jack cheese with jalapeño peppers, divided

2 tablespoons grated Parmesan cheese

1 teaspoon chili powder

¼ teaspoon salt

¼ teaspoon black pepper

¾ cup 1% low-fat milk

¼ cup chopped fresh cilantro

1 (11-ounce) can tomatillos, drained

1 (4.5-ounce) can chopped green chiles, drained

12 (6-inch) corn tortillas

Cooking spray

1. Preheat oven to 375°.

2. Combine cooked chicken, onions, ¼ cup Monterey Jack cheese, Parmesan, chili powder, salt, and pepper in a medium bowl. Place milk and next 3 ingredients in a food processor or blender; process until smooth.

3. Heat tortillas according to package directions. Pour ⅓ cup tomatillo mixture into bottom of an 11 x 7–inch baking dish coated with cooking spray. Arrange 4 corn tortillas in dish, and top with half of chicken mixture. Repeat layers with remaining tortillas and chicken mixture, ending with tortillas.

4. Pour remaining 1½ cups tomatillo mixture over tortillas; sprinkle with remaining ¼ cup Monterey Jack cheese. Bake at 375° for 20 minutes or until bubbly.

CALORIES 347; FAT 10.9g (sat 4.5g, mono 2.9g, poly 1.9g); PROTEIN 30.9g; CARB 33.3g; FIBER 5.9g; CHOL 79mg; IRON 1.5mg; SODIUM 560mg; CALC 272mg

Chicken Tamale Casserole

Homemade tamales are too time-consuming to prepare for weeknight meals; a corn muffin mix approximates the flavor.

Yield: 8 servings

1 cup (4 ounces) preshredded 4-cheese Mexican blend cheese, divided

⅓ cup fat-free milk

¼ cup egg substitute

1 teaspoon ground cumin

⅛ teaspoon ground red pepper

1 (14¾-ounce) can cream-style corn

1 (8.5-ounce) box corn muffin mix (such as Martha White)

1 (4-ounce) can chopped green chiles, drained

Cooking spray

1 (10-ounce) can red enchilada sauce (such as Old El Paso)

2 cups shredded cooked chicken breast

½ cup fat-free sour cream

Crushed red pepper (optional)

1. Preheat oven to 400°.

2. Combine ¼ cup cheese and next 7 ingredients in a large bowl, stirring just until moist. Pour mixture into a 13 x 9–inch baking dish coated with cooking spray.

3. Bake at 400° for 15 minutes or until set. Pierce entire surface liberally with a fork; pour enchilada sauce over top. Top with chicken; sprinkle with remaining ¾ cup cheese. Bake at 400° for 15 minutes or until cheese melts. Remove from oven; let stand 5 minutes. Cut into 8 pieces; top each serving with 1 tablespoon sour cream and, if desired, crushed red pepper.

CALORIES 354; FAT 14.1g (sat 7.1g, mono 3.3g, poly 1.2g); PROTEIN 18.9g; CARB 36.3g; FIBER 2.5g; CHOL 58mg; IRON 1.7mg; SODIUM 620mg; CALC 179mg

Black Bean and Chicken Chilaquiles

This Mexican entrée is usually prepared in a skillet, but our hearty version is baked. Refrigerate leftover chilaquiles in individual microwave-safe containers with tight-fitting lids. To reheat, drizzle with a tablespoon of water, and microwave just until thoroughly heated.

Yield: 6 servings (serving size: 1 [3½-inch] square)

Cooking spray

1 cup thinly sliced onion

5 garlic cloves, minced

2 cups shredded cooked chicken breast

1 (15-ounce) can black beans, rinsed and drained

1 cup fat-free, less-sodium chicken broth

1 (7¾-ounce) can salsa de chile fresco (such as El Pato)

15 (6-inch) corn tortillas, cut into 1-inch strips

1 cup (4 ounces) shredded queso blanco

1. Preheat oven to 450°.

2. Heat a large nonstick skillet over medium-high heat. Coat pan with cooking spray. Add onion; sauté 5 minutes or until lightly browned. Add garlic; sauté 1 minute. Add chicken; cook 30 seconds. Transfer mixture to a medium bowl; stir in beans. Add broth and salsa to pan; bring to a boil. Reduce heat, and simmer 5 minutes, stirring occasionally. Set aside.

3. Place half of tortilla strips in bottom of an 11 x 7–inch baking dish coated with cooking spray. Layer half of chicken mixture over tortilla strips; top with remaining tortilla strips and chicken mixture. Pour broth mixture evenly over chicken mixture. Sprinkle with cheese. Bake at 450° for 10 minutes or until tortillas are lightly browned and cheese is melted.

CALORIES 293; FAT 4.9g (sat 1.7g, mono 1.5g, poly 1.2g); PROTEIN 22.9g; CARB 40g; FIBER 5.9g; CHOL 46mg; IRON 2.3mg; SODIUM 602mg; CALC 200mg

Weeknight Coq au Vin

Serve this robust French classic over egg noodles to round out the meal.

Yield: 4 servings (serving size: 1 thigh, 1 drumstick, and ¾ cup sauce)

2 bacon slices, chopped

4 (4-ounce) bone-in chicken thighs, skinned

4 (4-ounce) chicken drumsticks, skinned

½ teaspoon salt

½ teaspoon freshly ground black pepper

¼ cup finely chopped fresh flat-leaf parsley, divided

1½ cups sliced cremini mushrooms

1½ cups dry red wine

1 cup chopped carrot

½ cup chopped shallots

½ cup fat-free, less-sodium chicken broth

1 tablespoon brandy

1 teaspoon minced fresh thyme

2 teaspoons tomato paste

1 garlic clove, minced

1. Cook bacon in a large Dutch oven over medium-high heat 2 minutes. Sprinkle chicken with salt and pepper. Add chicken to pan; cook 2 minutes. Stir in 3 tablespoons parsley, mushrooms, and remaining ingredients; bring to a boil. Cover, reduce heat, and simmer 25 minutes or until chicken is done.
2. Remove chicken with a slotted spoon; keep warm. Bring cooking liquid to a boil; cook until reduced to 3 cups (about 6 minutes). Return chicken to pan; cook 1 minute or until thoroughly heated. Sprinkle with remaining 1 tablespoon parsley.

CALORIES 345; FAT 12.7g (sat 3.7g, mono 4.7g, poly 2.7g); PROTEIN 43.7g; CARB 11g; FIBER 1.6g; CHOL 150mg; IRON 3.3mg; SODIUM 595mg; CALC 60mg

INGREDIENT TIP

A good rule of thumb when cooking with wine is to use a wine that is the same or has similar qualities to the wine you'll serve with the meal. For this traditional French dish, a dry red wine works well, particularly a Burgundy or pinot noir.

Chicken with Dark Beer

Residents of Southern France like their chicken cooked in wine, preferably a rich red, but those living in the North go for the caramel intensity of dark beer laced with plenty of onions. The sweetness of the beer is enhanced with a spicing of juniper berries and a shot of gin. The traditional accompaniment would be mashed or boiled potatoes.

Yield: 4 servings

3 tablespoons all-purpose flour

½ teaspoon salt

¼ teaspoon freshly ground black pepper

2 bone-in chicken breast halves, skinned

2 bone-in chicken thighs, skinned

2 chicken drumsticks, skinned

2 tablespoons butter

1 tablespoon canola oil

3 tablespoons dry gin

¾ cup chopped celery

¾ cup chopped peeled carrot

½ cup chopped shallots (about 3 medium)

3 juniper berries, crushed

1 (8-ounce) package mushrooms, halved

3 sprigs fresh thyme

3 sprigs fresh flat-leaf parsley

1 bay leaf

1 cup dark beer

¼ cup whole-milk Greek-style yogurt

2 teaspoons white wine vinegar

1 tablespoon chopped fresh flat-leaf parsley

1. Combine first 3 ingredients; sprinkle evenly over both sides of chicken. Heat butter and oil in a large, deep skillet over medium-high heat. Add chicken to pan; sauté 5 minutes on each side or until browned. Remove pan from heat. Pour gin into one side of pan; return pan to heat. Ignite gin with a long match; let flames die down. Remove chicken from pan; set aside and keep warm.

2. Add celery, carrot, shallots, and juniper berries to pan; sauté 5 minutes or until vegetables are tender, stirring occasionally. Add mushrooms. Place thyme, parsley, and bay leaf on a double layer of cheesecloth. Gather edges of cheesecloth together; tie securely. Add cheesecloth bag to pan. Return chicken to pan, nestling into vegetable mixture. Stir in beer; bring to a simmer. Cover, reduce heat, and simmer 45 minutes or until a thermometer inserted in the meaty parts of chicken registers 160°. (Breasts may cook more quickly. Check them after 35 minutes, and remove them when they're done; keep warm.)

3. Discard cheesecloth bag. Remove chicken from pan; keep warm. Place pan over medium heat; stir in yogurt. Cook 1 minute or until thoroughly heated (do not boil, as the yogurt may curdle). Remove from heat; stir in vinegar. Taste and adjust seasoning, if desired. Place 1 chicken breast half or 1 drumstick and 1 thigh on each of 4 plates; top each serving with about ¾ cup sauce and vegetable mixture. Sprinkle with chopped parsley.

CALORIES 370; FAT 16g (sat 6.6g, mono 5g, poly 3g); PROTEIN 30.8g; CARB 15.1g; FIBER 1.4g; CHOL 103mg; IRON 2mg; SODIUM 465mg; CALC 55mg

MAKE-AHEAD TIP

The chicken can be prepared ahead and refrigerated in its sauce up to three days or frozen up to one month. Thaw, reheat, and add the yogurt and vinegar before serving.

Braised Herb Chicken Thighs with Potatoes

Choose red-skin potatoes that are similar in size so they'll be done at the same time as the chicken.

Yield: 4 servings (serving size: 2 thighs and about 1⅓ cups vegetable mixture)

2 tablespoons all-purpose flour

2 teaspoons paprika

1 teaspoon salt

1 teaspoon dried thyme

1 teaspoon dried oregano

½ teaspoon black pepper

8 chicken thighs (about 2 pounds), skinned

1 teaspoon olive oil

1½ cups (2-inch-thick) slices carrot

1 large onion, cut into 8 wedges

1½ cups fat-free, less-sodium chicken broth

½ cup dry white wine

1½ pounds small red potatoes, quartered

1. Combine first 6 ingredients in a large zip-top plastic bag. Add chicken; seal bag, shaking to coat.
2. Heat oil in a Dutch oven over medium heat. Add chicken and remaining flour mixture to pan; cook 3 minutes on each side or until lightly brown. Add carrot and onion; cook 3 minutes, stirring frequently. Add broth, wine, and potatoes; bring to a boil. Reduce heat, and simmer 35 minutes or until chicken is done and vegetables are tender.

CALORIES 467; FAT 14.9g (sat 3.9g, mono 5.9g, poly 3.4g); PROTEIN 37.2g; CARB 40g; FIBER 5.7g; CHOL 115mg; IRON 4.4mg; SODIUM 887mg; CALC 71mg

INGREDIENT TIP

Sometimes called new potatoes, small, young red potatoes haven't had time to become starchy. Because of this, they have a waxy texture that makes them good for boiling and making potato salad, or for pan-roasting.

They are usually available from spring to early summer; use within two or three days after you purchase them.

Roasted Chicken Thighs Provençal

This recipe uses skinned, bone-in chicken thighs, which are meaty and succulent. Roasting the vegetables and chicken in one pan makes this an easy, one-dish meal.

Yield: 6 servings (serving size: 1 thigh, 1⅔ cups vegetable mixture, and 4 olives)

3 pounds small red potatoes, quartered

4 plum tomatoes, seeded and cut into 6 wedges

3 carrots, peeled and cut into 1-inch chunks

Cooking spray

1 tablespoon olive oil

1½ tablespoons chopped fresh rosemary, divided

2 teaspoons chopped fresh thyme, divided

1 teaspoon salt, divided

½ teaspoon freshly ground black pepper, divided

6 (6-ounce) skinless chicken thighs

24 niçoise olives

Rosemary sprigs (optional)

1. Preheat oven to 425°.

2. Place potatoes, tomatoes, and carrots on a jelly-roll pan coated with cooking spray. Drizzle vegetable mixture with olive oil; sprinkle with 1 tablespoon chopped rosemary, 1 teaspoon thyme, ¾ teaspoon salt, and ¼ teaspoon pepper. Toss gently, and spread into a single layer on pan. Bake at 425° for 30 minutes. Remove vegetable mixture from pan, and keep warm.

3. Sprinkle chicken with remaining 1½ teaspoons chopped rosemary, remaining 1 teaspoon thyme, remaining ¼ teaspoon salt, and remaining ¼ teaspoon pepper. Add chicken and olives to pan. Bake at 425° for 35 minutes or until chicken is done. Garnish with rosemary sprigs, if desired.

CALORIES 519; FAT 20.6g (sat 4.7g, mono 10g, poly 4g); PROTEIN 38.5g; CARB 43.5g; FIBER 5.5g; CHOL 121mg; IRON 3.7mg; SODIUM 786mg; CALC 67mg

INGREDIENT TIP

If you can't find niçoise olives, use kalamatas instead.

Mediterranean Chicken with Potatoes

The small red potatoes in this dish are roasted in the oven to give them a deep caramelized flavor before they're tossed with the other ingredients. A Greek salad makes a great side dish for this wonderful blend of flavors and textures. A crusty bread loaf and a good bottle of wine are all you need to round out this meal.

Yield: 8 servings (serving size: 1¼ cups)

4 teaspoons minced garlic, divided

1 tablespoon olive oil

1 teaspoon salt, divided

¼ teaspoon dried thyme

½ teaspoon black pepper, divided

12 small red potatoes, halved (about 1½ pounds)

Cooking spray

2 pounds skinless, boneless chicken breast, cut into bite-sized pieces

1 cup vertically sliced red onion

¾ cup dry white wine

¾ cup fat-free, less-sodium chicken broth

½ cup chopped pepperoncini peppers

¼ cup pitted kalamata olives, halved

2 cups chopped plum tomato

2 tablespoons chopped fresh basil

1 (14-ounce) can artichoke hearts, drained and quartered

½ cup (2 ounces) grated fresh Parmesan cheese

Thyme sprigs (optional)

1. Preheat oven to 400°.

2. Combine 2 teaspoons garlic, olive oil, ¼ teaspoon salt, thyme, ¼ teaspoon black pepper, and potatoes on a jelly-roll pan coated with cooking spray. Bake at 400° for 30 minutes or until tender.

3. Heat a large Dutch oven over medium-high heat. Coat pan with cooking spray. Sprinkle chicken with ½ teaspoon salt and ¼ teaspoon black pepper. Add half of chicken to pan; sauté 5 minutes or until browned. Remove chicken from pan. Repeat procedure with remaining chicken; remove from pan.

4. Add onion to pan; sauté 5 minutes. Stir in wine, scraping pan to loosen browned bits. Bring wine to a boil; cook until reduced to ⅓ cup (about 2 minutes). Add potatoes, chicken, broth, pepperoncini, and olives; cook 3 minutes, stirring occasionally. Stir in 2 teaspoons garlic, remaining ¼ teaspoon salt, tomato, basil, and artichokes; cook 3 minutes or until thoroughly heated. Sprinkle with cheese. Garnish with thyme sprigs, if desired.

CALORIES 331; FAT 7.3g (sat 2.1g, mono 3.7g, poly 0.9g); PROTEIN 33.5g; CARB 32.5g; FIBER 3.6g; CHOL 71mg; IRON 2.9mg; SODIUM 897mg; CALC 124mg

Chicken Thighs with Olives and Tomato Sauce

Add capers along with the olives, parsley, and seasoning for a more briny flavor, if you like. The parsley goes in last to keep its flavor and color intense.

Yield: 6 servings (serving size: 2 thighs and about ⅓ cup sauce)

12 chicken thighs (about 4 pounds), skinned

1 teaspoon kosher salt, divided

¼ teaspoon freshly ground black pepper, divided

1 teaspoon olive oil

1½ tablespoons minced garlic

¼ cup dry white wine

3 tablespoons tomato paste

2 to 3 teaspoons crushed red pepper

1 (28-ounce) can diced tomatoes, drained

¼ cup sliced pitted kalamata olives

2 tablespoons chopped fresh flat-leaf parsley

1. Sprinkle chicken with ½ teaspoon salt and ⅛ teaspoon black pepper. Heat oil in a large skillet over medium-high heat. Add chicken to pan; cook 2 minutes on each side or until browned. Place chicken in an electric slow cooker. Add garlic to pan, and sauté 30 seconds, stirring constantly. Add wine, scraping pan to loosen browned bits; cook 30 seconds. Place wine mixture in cooker. Add tomato paste, crushed red pepper, and tomatoes to cooker. Cover and cook on HIGH 4 hours. Stir in remaining ½ teaspoon salt, remaining ⅛ teaspoon pepper, olives, and parsley.

CALORIES 270; FAT 12.9g (sat 3.3g, mono 5.6g, poly 2.8g); PROTEIN 29.1g; CARB 8.7g; FIBER 2.2g; CHOL 99mg; IRON 2.4mg; SODIUM 658mg; CALC 44mg

EQUIPMENT TIP

A slow cooker is a boon to a busy cook because it does most of the work for you—it cooks dinner while you're away. By the day's end, you have a home-cooked meal ready and waiting.

Chicken and Root Vegetable Potpie

In the magazine's early days, we shied away from indulgent ingredients like puff pastry. Now, though, we understand that these items can fit into a healthful diet. This dish registers at just 30 percent calories from fat—root vegetables help balance the fat from the flaky topping. Garnish with fresh thyme sprigs, if desired.

Yield: 8 servings

3 cups fat-free, less-sodium chicken broth

1½ cups frozen green peas, thawed

1 cup (½-inch) cubed peeled baking potato

1 cup (½-inch) cubed peeled sweet potato

1 cup (½-inch) cubed peeled celeriac (celery root)

1 cup (½-inch-thick) slices parsnip

1 (10-ounce) package frozen pearl onions

1 pound skinless, boneless chicken breast, cut into bite-sized pieces

3 ounces all-purpose flour (about ⅔ cup), divided

1½ cups fat-free milk

¼ cup chopped fresh parsley

2 tablespoons chopped fresh thyme

1½ teaspoons salt

1 teaspoon freshly ground black pepper

Cooking spray

1 sheet frozen puff pastry dough, thawed

1. Preheat oven to 400°.

2. Bring broth to a boil in a large Dutch oven. Add peas and next 5 ingredients to pan; cover, reduce heat, and simmer 6 minutes. Add chicken; cook 5 minutes or until chicken is done. Remove chicken and vegetables from broth with a slotted spoon; place in a large bowl.

3. Increase heat to medium. Lightly spoon flour into a dry measuring cup; level with a knife. Place all but 1 tablespoon flour in a medium bowl; gradually add milk to bowl, stirring with a whisk until well blended. Add milk mixture to broth; cook 5 minutes or until thickened, stirring frequently. Stir in chicken mixture, parsley, thyme, salt, and pepper. Spoon mixture into an 11 x 7–inch baking dish coated with cooking spray.

4. Sprinkle remaining 1 tablespoon flour on a work surface; roll dough into a 13 x 9–inch rectangle. Place dough over chicken mixture, pressing to seal at edges of dish. Cut small slits into dough to allow steam to escape; coat dough lightly with cooking spray. Place dish on a foil-lined baking sheet. Bake at 400° for 16 minutes or until pastry is browned and filling is bubbly.

CALORIES 388; FAT 13g (sat 2g, mono 3g, poly 7.1g); PROTEIN 21.9g; CARB 45.7g; FIBER 4.4g; CHOL 34mg; IRON 3mg; SODIUM 790mg; CALC 115mg

EQUIPMENT TIP

This recipe calls for a baking dish, but you can use 8 (10-ounce) ramekins, if you prefer.

Herbed Chicken and Dumplings

Fluffy herb-flecked dumplings, tender vegetables, and rich dark-meat chicken combine in this soul-satisfying comfort dish. Garnish each serving with a fresh sprig of parsley, if desired. This is a perfect, cozy dinner for two on a chilly night.

Yield: 2 servings (serving size: 2 cups)

Cooking spray

8 ounces skinless, boneless chicken thighs, cut into bite-sized pieces

¾ cup (¼-inch) diagonally cut celery

½ cup (¼-inch) diagonally cut carrot

½ cup chopped onion

⅛ teaspoon dried thyme

3 fresh parsley sprigs

1 bay leaf

3 cups fat-free, less-sodium chicken broth

2.25 ounces all-purpose flour (about ½ cup)

1 tablespoon chopped fresh parsley

¼ teaspoon baking powder

¼ teaspoon salt

¼ cup 1% low-fat milk

1. Heat a large saucepan over medium-high heat. Coat pan with cooking spray. Add chicken to pan; cook 4 minutes, browning on all sides. Remove chicken from pan; keep warm. Add celery and next 5 ingredients to pan; sauté 5 minutes or until onion is tender. Return chicken to pan; cook 1 minute. Add broth to pan; bring mixture to a boil. Cover, reduce heat, and simmer 30 minutes.

2. Lightly spoon flour into a dry measuring cup; level with a knife. Combine flour, chopped parsley, baking powder, and salt in a medium bowl. Add milk, stirring just until moist. Spoon by heaping teaspoonfuls into broth mixture; cover and simmer 10 minutes or until dumplings are done. Discard parsley sprigs and bay leaf.

CALORIES 285; FAT 5.2g (sat 1.5g, mono 1.9g, poly 1.2g); PROTEIN 25g; CARB 35.2g; FIBER 3.1g; CHOL 55mg; IRON 3.4mg; SODIUM 596mg; CALC 133mg

Country Captain Chicken

Both South Carolina and Georgia lay claim to this Southern classic, which may have been brought to America by a ship's captain ferrying spices from the Far East. If desired, top each serving with 1 tablespoon bottled mango chutney. Rice is a traditional side dish.

Yield: 4 servings (serving size: 1½ cups chicken mixture and 2 tablespoons almonds)

1 tablespoon curry powder

¼ teaspoon salt

¼ teaspoon black pepper

1 pound skinless, boneless chicken breast, cut into ¾-inch pieces

1½ tablespoons olive oil

2½ cups vertically sliced onion (about 2 medium)

¾ cup thinly sliced green bell pepper (about 1 medium)

2 garlic cloves, minced

⅔ cup fat-free, less-sodium chicken broth

¼ cup dried currants

2 tablespoons chopped fresh thyme, divided

1 (14.5-ounce) can diced tomatoes with jalapeño, undrained

½ cup sliced almonds, toasted

1. Combine curry powder, salt, and black pepper. Sprinkle chicken with curry mixture.

2. Heat oil in a large nonstick skillet over medium-high heat. Add chicken mixture to pan; sauté 5 minutes. Add onion, bell pepper, and garlic; sauté 3 minutes. Add broth, currants, 1 tablespoon thyme, and tomatoes; bring to a boil. Reduce heat, and simmer 5 minutes. Stir in remaining 1 tablespoon thyme; cook 1 minute. Sprinkle with almonds.

CALORIES 314; FAT 11.2g (sat 1.4g, mono 7g, poly 1.9g); PROTEIN 30.5g; CARB 23.2g; FIBER 4.6g; CHOL 66mg; IRON 2.6mg; SODIUM 683mg; CALC 86mg

QUICK TIP

To make it fast, cook 1 (3½-ounce) bag boil-in-bag rice, omitting salt and fat. Stir in ¼ teaspoon salt and ¼ teaspoon black pepper.

Sherry-Soy Glazed Chicken

Pair this entrée with a simple rice pilaf: Heat 1 tablespoon canola oil in a large saucepan over medium-high heat. Add ½ cup chopped onion and 2 teaspoons grated peeled fresh ginger to pan; sauté 2 minutes. Stir in 1 cup water, ½ cup long-grain rice, and ¼ teaspoon salt; bring to a boil. Cover, reduce heat, and simmer 12 minutes or until liquid is absorbed. Remove from heat; stir in 2 tablespoons chopped fresh cilantro.

Yield: 4 servings (serving size: about ¾ cup)

3 tablespoons low-sodium soy sauce, divided

2 tablespoons dry sherry

4 teaspoons cornstarch, divided

1 pound skinless, boneless chicken breast, cut into bite-sized pieces

½ cup fat-free, less-sodium chicken broth

2 tablespoons oyster sauce

1 tablespoon honey

2 teaspoons sesame oil, divided

¾ cup chopped onion

½ cup chopped celery

½ cup chopped red bell pepper

1 tablespoon grated peeled fresh ginger

2 garlic cloves, minced

½ cup chopped green onions (about 3 green onions)

¼ cup chopped unsalted dry-roasted cashews

1. Combine 1 tablespoon soy sauce, sherry, 2 teaspoons cornstarch, and chicken in a bowl; toss well to coat. Combine remaining 2 tablespoons soy sauce, remaining 2 teaspoons cornstarch, broth, oyster sauce, and honey in a small bowl.

2. Heat 1 teaspoon oil in a large nonstick skillet over medium-high heat. Add chicken mixture to pan; sauté 3 minutes. Remove from pan. Heat remaining 1 teaspoon oil in pan. Add onion, celery, and bell pepper to pan; sauté 2 minutes. Add ginger and garlic; sauté 1 minute. Stir in broth mixture. Bring to a boil; cook 1 minute, stirring constantly. Remove from heat. Return chicken to pan. Sprinkle with green onions and cashews.

CALORIES 257; FAT 9g (sat 1.9g, mono 4.2g, poly 2.3g); PROTEIN 26g; CARB 17g; FIBER 1.9g; CHOL 63mg; IRON 2mg; SODIUM 584mg; CALC 45mg

Spicy Asian Noodles with Chicken

Add a snow pea sauté to complete the meal: Heat 2 teaspoons canola oil in a large nonstick skillet over medium-high heat. Add 2 minced garlic cloves; sauté 15 seconds. Add 2 cups trimmed fresh snow peas and 1 cup drained sliced canned water chestnuts; sauté 3 minutes or until crisp-tender. Remove from heat; stir in 1 tablespoon low-sodium soy sauce.

Yield: 4 servings (serving size: 1¾ cups)

1 tablespoon dark sesame oil, divided

1 tablespoon grated peeled fresh ginger

2 garlic cloves, minced

2 cups chopped roasted chicken breast

½ cup chopped green onions

¼ cup chopped fresh cilantro

3 tablespoons low-sodium soy sauce

2 tablespoons rice vinegar

2 tablespoons hoisin sauce

2 teaspoons sambal oelek (ground fresh chile paste)

1 (6.75-ounce) package thin rice sticks (rice-flour noodles)

2 tablespoons chopped dry-roasted peanuts

1. Heat 2 teaspoons oil in a small skillet over medium-high heat. Add ginger and garlic to pan; cook 45 seconds, stirring constantly. Place in a large bowl. Stir in remaining 1 teaspoon oil, chicken, and next 6 ingredients.

2. Cook noodles according to package directions. Drain and rinse under cold water; drain. Cut noodles into smaller pieces. Add noodles to bowl; toss well to coat. Sprinkle with peanuts.

CALORIES 381; FAT 8.1g (sat 1.5g, mono 3.2g, poly 2.7g); PROTEIN 27.5g; CARB 47.1g; FIBER 2.3g; CHOL 60mg; IRON 3.1mg; SODIUM 614mg; CALC 55mg

Curried Chicken and Cashews

Madras curry powder delivers more intensity than regular curry powder. For less heat, leave the chiles whole when you add them to the wok with the curry powder.

Yield: 4 servings (serving size: 1 cup chicken mixture and ¾ cup rice)

Sauce:

⅓ cup fat-free, less-sodium chicken broth

3 tablespoons water

1½ tablespoons fish sauce

1 teaspoon sugar

1 teaspoon rice vinegar

Remaining Ingredients:

¾ pound skinless, boneless chicken breast

2 tablespoons canola oil, divided

1½ cups vertically sliced onion

1 tablespoon minced peeled fresh ginger

1 tablespoon minced garlic

1 teaspoon Madras curry powder

3 small dried hot red chiles, broken in half

⅓ cup chopped fresh cilantro

¼ cup dry-roasted salted cashews, chopped

3 cups hot cooked short-grain rice

1. To prepare sauce, combine first 5 ingredients; set aside.

2. Cut chicken across grain into ¼-inch slices; cut slices into ½-inch-wide strips. Cut strips into 3-inch-long pieces.

3. Heat a 14-inch wok over high heat. Add 1 tablespoon oil to wok, swirling to coat. Add half of chicken to wok; stir-fry 2 minutes. Spoon cooked chicken into a bowl. Repeat procedure with 2 teaspoons oil and remaining chicken.

4. Add remaining 1 teaspoon oil to wok, swirling to coat. Add onion, ginger, and garlic to wok; stir-fry 1 minute or until lightly browned. Add curry powder and chiles; stir-fry 30 seconds. Add sauce and chicken to wok; stir-fry 1 minute. Spoon into a serving dish. Sprinkle with cilantro and cashews. Serve over rice.

CALORIES 439; FAT 13g (sat 1.7g, mono 6.9g, poly 3.2g); PROTEIN 26g; CARB 52.6g; FIBER 3.2g; CHOL 49mg; IRON 3.9mg; SODIUM 669mg; CALC 37mg

INGREDIENT TIP

Madras curry powder, named for a city in southern India, is hotter than standard curry powder. It quickly loses its pungency, so store it in an airtight container, and use it within two months.

Rosemary Chicken and White Beans

A spinach salad spiked with slivered red onions and drizzled with red wine vinaigrette complements this dish nicely.

Yield: 4 servings (serving size: 2 thighs and ¾ cup bean mixture)

2 teaspoons olive oil

1½ teaspoons dried rosemary

¼ teaspoon salt

¼ teaspoon black pepper

8 skinless, boneless chicken thighs (about 1 pound)

1 (14.5-ounce) can stewed tomatoes, undrained

1 (15-ounce) can navy beans, drained

¼ cup chopped pitted kalamata olives

1. Heat olive oil in a large skillet over medium-high heat. Combine rosemary, salt, and pepper; sprinkle over one side of chicken. Place chicken in pan, seasoned side down; cook 3 minutes. Reduce heat to medium; turn chicken. Add tomatoes and beans; cover and simmer 10 minutes or until chicken is done. Stir in olives.

CALORIES 316; FAT 8.1g (sat 1.7g, mono 3.7g, poly 1.5g); PROTEIN 31.2g; CARB 30.2g; FIBER 6.8g; CHOL 94mg; IRON 4.2mg; SODIUM 978mg; CALC 109mg

INGREDIENT TIP

Skinless, boneless chicken thighs are widely available. If your fresh-meat counter doesn't carry them, check the freezer case for bargain-sized bags of individually frozen portions.

Barley, Wild Rice, and Chicken Pilaf

This recipe has some of the creamy texture of a risotto but requires far less stirring.

Yield: 4 servings (serving size: 1 cup)

½ cup hot water

¼ cup dried porcini mushrooms, chopped

1 tablespoon olive oil

1 cup finely chopped onion (about 1 medium)

3 garlic cloves, minced

¾ cup uncooked pearl barley

¼ cup wild rice

2 teaspoons chopped fresh thyme

1 (14-ounce) can fat-free, less-sodium chicken broth

2 cups chopped cooked chicken breast

½ cup (2 ounces) grated fresh Parmesan cheese

¼ cup chopped fresh parsley

¼ teaspoon salt

¼ teaspoon freshly ground black pepper

1. Combine ½ cup hot water and mushrooms; let stand 10 minutes or until mushrooms are tender. Set aside.

2. Heat oil in a large nonstick skillet over medium heat. Add onion; cook 1 minute, stirring frequently. Add garlic; cook 30 seconds, stirring frequently. Add barley, rice, and thyme; cook 5 minutes or until lightly browned, stirring frequently. Stir in mushroom mixture and broth. Cover, reduce heat, and simmer 40 minutes or until barley is tender. Stir in chicken and cheese; cook 5 minutes or until thoroughly heated. Stir in parsley, salt, and pepper.

CALORIES 409; FAT 12.4g (sat 3.9g, mono 5.6g, poly 2g); PROTEIN 31.6g; CARB 42.8g; FIBER 7.7g; CHOL 68mg; IRON 2.7mg; SODIUM 515mg; CALC 160mg

WINE TIP

A chicken breast does not always demand to be paired with white wine, especially when it's accompanied by porcini mushrooms and wild rice. Serve an easy-drinking wine, like a pinot noir.

Chicken Biryani

Morsels of chicken are simmered until they're tender in this spicy Indian rice-based dish. Serve with a simple salad of thinly sliced cucumber and plum tomato wedges topped with yogurt dressing: Combine ⅓ cup plain low-fat yogurt, 1 tablespoon chopped green onions, 1 teaspoon fresh lemon juice, ¼ teaspoon ground cumin, ⅛ teaspoon salt, and a dash of ground red pepper.

Yield: 4 servings (serving size: 1½ cups rice mixture, 1 tablespoon almonds, and 1 lime wedge)

2 teaspoons canola oil

1 pound skinless, boneless chicken breast, cut into 1-inch pieces

1 cup chopped onion (about 1 medium)

1 jalapeño pepper, seeded and minced

1 teaspoon minced fresh ginger

1½ teaspoons garam masala

¾ teaspoon ground cumin

½ teaspoon salt

2 garlic cloves, minced

2 cups chopped plum tomato (about 2 tomatoes)

1 cup uncooked basmati rice

⅓ cup golden raisins

1 (14-ounce) can fat-free, less-sodium chicken broth

¼ cup chopped fresh cilantro

¼ cup sliced almonds

4 lime wedges

1. Heat oil in a large nonstick skillet over medium-high heat. Add chicken to pan; sauté 3 minutes. Add onion and jalapeño; sauté 3 minutes. Add ginger, garam masala, cumin, salt, and garlic; sauté 30 seconds. Add tomato, rice, raisins, and broth; bring to a boil. Cover, reduce heat, and simmer 15 minutes or until rice is tender. Stir in cilantro. Sprinkle with almonds; serve with lime wedges.

CALORIES 437; FAT 9.1g (sat 1.4g, mono 4.6g, poly 2.3g); PROTEIN 29.8g; CARB 63.2g; FIBER 4.5g; CHOL 66mg; IRON 3.4mg; SODIUM 555mg; CALC 58mg

Chicken and Shrimp Jambalaya

Try this dish when you're serving a crowd. Garnish with fresh flat-leaf parsley sprigs, if desired.

Yield: 8 servings (serving size: 1¼ cups)

1 tablespoon canola oil

1 pound skinless, boneless chicken breast, cut into 1-inch pieces

¾ pound skinless, boneless chicken thighs, cut into 1-inch pieces

2 cups chopped onion

1 cup chopped green bell pepper

1 cup chopped celery

2 garlic cloves, minced

4 ounces turkey kielbasa, halved and cut into ¼-inch-thick slices

2 teaspoons salt-free Cajun seasoning

½ teaspoon dried thyme

¼ teaspoon Spanish smoked paprika (optional)

2 (14½-ounce) cans diced tomatoes with onion, celery, and green peppers

1 (14-ounce) can fat-free, less-sodium chicken broth

2 (3½-ounce) bags boil-in-bag long-grain rice

1 pound medium shrimp, peeled and deveined

2 tablespoons chopped fresh flat-leaf parsley

1 tablespoon hot sauce

1. Heat oil in a large skillet over high heat. Add chicken; cook 4 minutes, stirring occasionally. Spoon chicken into an electric slow cooker.

2. Add onion, bell pepper, celery, and garlic to pan; sauté 4 minutes or until tender. Add onion mixture, turkey kielbasa, and next 5 ingredients to slow cooker. Cover and cook on LOW 5 hours.

3. Cook rice according to package directions. Add cooked rice and remaining ingredients to slow cooker. Cover and cook on HIGH 15 minutes or until the shrimp are done.

CALORIES 364; FAT 6.3g (sat 1.4g, mono 2g, poly 1.6g); PROTEIN 39.5g; CARB 34.8g; FIBER 3.5g; CHOL 157mg; IRON 4.8mg; SODIUM 727mg; CALC 110mg

grill it up

Chicken Shawarma

Shawarma is a Middle Eastern dish of garlicky meat or poultry served on pitas. From start to finish, you can have this on the table in 45 minutes.

Yield: 4 servings

Chicken:

2 tablespoons fresh lemon juice

1 teaspoon curry powder

2 teaspoons extra-virgin olive oil

¾ teaspoon salt

½ teaspoon ground cumin

3 garlic cloves, minced

1 pound skinless, boneless chicken breast, cut into 16 (3-inch) strips

Sauce:

½ cup plain 2% reduced-fat Greek yogurt (such as Fage)

2 tablespoons tahini

2 teaspoons fresh lemon juice

¼ teaspoon salt

1 garlic clove, minced

Remaining Ingredients:

Cooking spray

4 (6-inch) pitas

1 cup chopped romaine lettuce

8 (¼-inch-thick) tomato slices

1. Preheat grill to medium-high heat.

2. To prepare chicken, combine first 6 ingredients in a medium bowl. Add chicken to bowl; toss well to coat. Let stand at room temperature 20 minutes.

3. To prepare sauce, combine yogurt and next 4 ingredients, stirring with a whisk.

4. Thread 2 chicken strips onto each of 8 (12-inch) skewers. Place kebabs on grill rack coated with cooking spray; grill 4 minutes on each side or until done.

5. Place pitas on grill rack; grill 1 minute on each side or until lightly toasted. Place 1 pita on each of 4 plates; top each serving with ¼ cup lettuce and 2 tomato slices. Top each serving with 4 chicken pieces; drizzle each serving with 2 tablespoons sauce.

CALORIES 384; FAT 9.8g (sat 2.1g, mono 4.1g, poly 2.7g); PROTEIN 34.4g; CARB 40g; FIBER 2.5g; CHOL 64mg; IRON 4.3mg; SODIUM 821mg; CALC 106mg

Chicken Skewers with Soy-Mirin Marinade

This marinade would also pair nicely with salmon. Serve with sautéed snow peas.

Yield: 4 servings (serving size: 2 skewers and ¾ cup rice)

⅓ cup mirin (sweet rice wine)

⅓ cup low-sodium soy sauce

1 teaspoon dark sesame oil

1½ pounds skinless, boneless chicken breast halves, cut lengthwise into 1-inch strips

1 large red bell pepper, cut into 8 pieces

1 large green bell pepper, cut into 8 pieces

Cooking spray

2 tablespoons sesame seeds, toasted

3 cups hot cooked rice

1. Combine first 3 ingredients in a large bowl; add chicken to bowl, and toss to coat. Let stand 15 minutes, turning chicken occasionally.
2. Prepare grill.
3. Remove chicken from bag, reserving marinade. Place marinade in a small saucepan; bring to a boil. Cook until reduced to ¼ cup (about 5 minutes). Thread chicken and bell peppers on 8 (12-inch) wooden skewers. Brush skewers with marinade. Place skewers on grill rack coated with cooking spray. Grill 4 minutes on each side or until done, brushing occasionally with remaining marinade. Remove from grill; sprinkle with sesame seeds. Serve with rice.

CALORIES 463; FAT 8.5g (sat 1.8g, mono 2.4g, poly 1.9g); PROTEIN 44.9g; CARB 44.5g; FIBER 3.1g; CHOL 108mg; IRON 4.6mg; SODIUM 814mg; CALC 46mg

SAFETY TIP

Soak wooden skewers in water for at least 30 minutes before using them or they'll burn.

Wooden skewers should be discarded after use. If you grill often, invest in a set of metal skewers, which can be reused and won't require soaking.

Spiedini of Chicken and Zucchini with Almond Salsa Verde

Spiedini is Italian for "little skewers." These grilled kebabs are paired with a zesty sauce of herbs, nuts, citrus, and capers.

Yield: 6 servings (serving size: 2 spiedini and 2½ tablespoons salsa)

Salsa:

1 cup chopped fresh parsley

2 tablespoons chopped almonds, toasted

2 tablespoons chopped fresh chives

3 tablespoons capers, chopped

½ teaspoon grated lemon rind

3 tablespoons fresh lemon juice

1 tablespoon extra-virgin olive oil

½ teaspoon chopped fresh thyme

½ teaspoon chopped fresh oregano

¼ teaspoon kosher salt

⅛ teaspoon freshly ground black pepper

1 garlic clove, minced

Spiedini:

1½ pounds skinless, boneless chicken breast, cut into 1-inch pieces

6 small zucchini, cut into 1-inch slices (about 1¼ pounds)

Cooking spray

¼ teaspoon kosher salt

⅛ teaspoon freshly ground black pepper

1. Soak 12 (10-inch) wooden skewers in water 30 minutes to prevent burning.

2. Prepare grill to medium-high heat.

3. To prepare salsa, combine first 12 ingredients; set aside.

4. To prepare spiedini, thread chicken and zucchini alternately onto each of 12 (10-inch) skewers. Coat spiedini with cooking spray; sprinkle evenly with ¼ teaspoon salt and ⅛ teaspoon pepper. Place on grill rack; grill 6 minutes or until done, turning once. Serve with salsa.

CALORIES 187; FAT 5.5g (sat 0.9g, mono 2.9g, poly 1.1g); PROTEIN 28.7g; CARB 6.3g; FIBER 2.2g; CHOL 66mg; IRON 2.1mg; SODIUM 376mg; CALC 56mg

MAKE-AHEAD TIP

For a backyard barbecue, prepare the salsa up to a day ahead, and assemble the skewers earlier in the day. Coat with cooking spray and seasonings just before grilling.

Grilled Chicken and Lemon Salad

Depending on the season, you may want to consider substituting thin, blanched, fresh asparagus for the sugar snap peas. You can't go wrong with either application.

Yield: 4 servings

Chicken:

¾ cup fresh lemon juice

¼ cup olive oil

1 tablespoon fresh thyme leaves

1 teaspoon salt

4 (6-ounce) skinless, boneless chicken breast halves

Cooking spray

Salad:

1 cup sugar snap peas, trimmed

½ cup red bell pepper strips

½ cup yellow bell pepper strips

½ cup (¼-inch-thick) slices zucchini

2 tablespoons chopped fresh cilantro

1 tablespoon extra-virgin olive oil

¼ teaspoon salt

¼ teaspoon freshly ground black pepper

4 lemon wedges (optional)

1. To prepare chicken, combine first 4 ingredients in a large zip-top plastic bag. Add chicken to bag, and seal. Marinate in refrigerator 1 hour, turning occasionally.

2. Prepare grill.

3. Remove chicken from bag; discard marinade. Place chicken on grill rack coated with cooking spray; grill 6 minutes on each side or until done. Cool completely; cut into ¼-inch-thick slices.

4. To prepare salad, cook peas in boiling water 30 seconds. Drain, and rinse with cold water. Drain. Combine peas and next 7 ingredients in a large bowl; add chicken, tossing to combine. Place 1¾ cups chicken salad on each of 4 plates. Serve with lemon wedges, if desired.

CALORIES 259; FAT 7.1g (sat 1.2g, mono 4g, poly 1g); PROTEIN 40.5g; CARB 5.3g; FIBER 0.8g; CHOL 99mg; IRON 1.5mg; SODIUM 332mg; CALC 35mg

FLAVOR TIP

Freshly squeezed lemon juice is essential to the flavor of this salad. It makes a world of difference. The bottled juice just doesn't compare. Microwave lemons for about 30 seconds before squeezing them; they'll yield more juice.

Grilled Chicken and Pesto Farfalle

Garnish with basil sprigs, if desired. If you serve wine, a chardonnay complements the creamy sauce.

Yield: 10 servings (serving size: 2 cups pasta mixture and about 1½ tablespoons cheese)

1¾ pounds skinless, boneless chicken breast halves

1 teaspoon salt, divided

¾ teaspoon freshly ground black pepper, divided

Cooking spray

20 ounces uncooked farfalle (bow tie pasta)

1 tablespoon butter

3 garlic cloves, minced

1½ cups 1% low-fat milk, divided

2 tablespoons all-purpose flour

1 (3.5-ounce) jar commercial pesto (about ⅓ cup)

¾ cup half-and-half

2 cups (8 ounces) shredded fresh Parmesan cheese, divided

4 cups halved grape tomatoes (about 2 pints)

½ cup chopped fresh basil

1. Prepare grill to medium-high heat.

2. Sprinkle chicken evenly with ¼ teaspoon salt and ¼ teaspoon pepper. Place chicken on grill rack coated with cooking spray; grill 10 minutes or until done, turning after 6 minutes. Remove from grill; let stand 5 minutes. Cut chicken into ½-inch pieces; keep warm.

3. Cook pasta according to package directions, omitting salt and fat. Drain in colander over a bowl, reserving ¼ cup cooking liquid. Place pasta in large bowl.

4. Heat butter in a medium saucepan over medium heat. Add garlic to pan; cook 1 minute, stirring occasionally. Combine ½ cup milk and flour in a small bowl, stirring with a whisk. Add milk mixture to pan, stirring constantly with a whisk. Stir in pesto. Gradually add remaining 1 cup milk and half-and-half, stirring constantly with a whisk. Cook 8 minutes or until sauce thickens, stirring frequently. Add ¼ cup reserved cooking liquid, remaining ¾ teaspoon salt, remaining ½ teaspoon pepper, and 1 cup cheese; stir until cheese melts.

5. Add chicken and sauce to pasta, tossing well to coat. Add tomatoes and basil; toss gently. Sprinkle with remaining 1 cup cheese. Serve immediately.

CALORIES 508; FAT 16.7g (sat 7.7g, mono 6.5g, poly 1.1g); PROTEIN 38.3g; CARB 50.7g; FIBER 2.9g; CHOL 81mg; IRON 3.5mg; SODIUM 781mg; CALC 397mg

QUICK TIP

This dish comes together quickly if one person grills the chicken while another cooks the pasta and sauce.

Lemon-Grilled Chicken Breasts

To round out your meal, serve this versatile grilled chicken with a couscous and pine nut pilaf and grilled asparagus. Garnish with grilled lemon slices, if desired.

Yield: 7 servings (serving size: 1 chicken breast half)

3 tablespoons fresh lemon juice

2 tablespoons extra-virgin olive oil

2 garlic cloves, minced

7 (6-ounce) skinless, boneless chicken breast halves

½ teaspoon kosher salt

½ teaspoon freshly ground black pepper

Cooking spray

1. Prepare grill to medium-high heat.

2. Combine first 4 ingredients in a large zip-top plastic bag; seal. Marinate in refrigerator 30 minutes, turning occasionally. Remove chicken from bag; discard marinade. Sprinkle chicken evenly with salt and pepper.

3. Place chicken on grill rack coated with cooking spray; grill 6 minutes on each side or until done.

CALORIES 159; FAT 3.5g (sat 0.7g, mono 1.8g, poly 0.6g); PROTEIN 29.5g; CARB 0.5g; FIBER 0.1g; CHOL 74mg; IRON 1mg; SODIUM 218mg; CALC 16mg

Grilled Chicken with Fruit Salsa

Combine lemon juice, soy sauce, fresh ginger, lemon pepper, and garlic to make a kickin' marinade for grilled chicken. Fruit salsa adds sweetness and crunch to this tropical dish.

Yield: 6 servings (serving size: 1 chicken breast half and ½ cup salsa)

Chicken:

½ cup fresh lemon juice (about 4 lemons)

½ cup low-sodium soy sauce

1 tablespoon minced peeled fresh ginger

1 tablespoon lemon pepper

2 garlic cloves, minced

6 (6-ounce) skinless, boneless chicken breast halves

Cooking spray

Salsa:

1½ cups cubed pineapple

¾ cup cubed peeled kiwifruit (about 3 kiwifruit)

¾ cup coarsely chopped orange sections

½ cup chopped peeled mango

½ cup diced red onion

2 tablespoons chopped fresh cilantro

1½ teaspoons ground cumin

¼ teaspoon salt

⅛ teaspoon black pepper

1 small jalapeño pepper, seeded and chopped

1. To prepare chicken, combine juice, soy sauce, ginger, lemon pepper, and garlic in a large zip-top plastic bag. Add chicken to bag; seal and shake to coat. Marinate in refrigerator 1 hour, turning once.

2. Prepare grill or broiler.

3. Remove chicken from bag; discard marinade. Place chicken on grill rack or broiler pan coated with cooking spray; cook 5 minutes on each side or until chicken is done.

4. To prepare salsa, combine pineapple and remaining ingredients, tossing gently. Serve with chicken.

CALORIES 257; FAT 2.6g (sat 0.6g, mono 0.6g, poly 0.6g); PROTEIN 40.9g; CARB 16.7g; FIBER 2.7g; CHOL 99mg; IRON 2mg; SODIUM 683mg; CALC 49mg

Grilled Cumin Chicken with Fresh Tomatillo Sauce

Bring the heat of the Southwest to the weeknight dinner table with this delicious take on chicken. Serve with chipotle rice. Combine 1 cup long-grain rice and 2 cups fat-free, less-sodium chicken broth in a medium saucepan; bring to a boil. Cover, reduce heat, and simmer 15 minutes or until liquid is absorbed. Stir in ¼ cup thinly sliced green onions and ½ teaspoon minced chipotle chile, canned in adobo sauce.

Yield: 4 servings (serving size: 1 chicken breast half and about 5 tablespoons sauce)

2 teaspoons olive oil

½ teaspoon ground cumin

⅛ teaspoon freshly ground black pepper

2 garlic cloves, minced

4 (6-ounce) skinless, boneless chicken breast halves

½ pound tomatillos

½ cup fat-free, less-sodium chicken broth

¼ cup cilantro leaves

¼ cup chopped green onions

2 tablespoons fresh lime juice

½ teaspoon sugar

¼ teaspoon salt

1 garlic clove, chopped

1 jalapeño pepper, seeded and chopped

¼ teaspoon salt

Cooking spray

1. Prepare grill to medium-high heat.
2. Combine first 4 ingredients in a large zip-top plastic bag. Add chicken to bag; seal and let stand 15 minutes.
3. Discard husks and stems from tomatillos. Combine tomatillos and broth in a small saucepan over medium-high heat; cover and cook 8 minutes. Drain and cool slightly. Place tomatillos, cilantro, and next 6 ingredients in a food processor; process until smooth.
4. Remove chicken from bag; discard marinade. Sprinkle chicken evenly with ¼ teaspoon salt. Place on a grill rack coated with cooking spray; grill 6 minutes on each side or until chicken is done. Serve with tomatillo sauce.

CALORIES 237; FAT 5.1g (sat 1g, mono 2.3g, poly 1g); PROTEIN 40.4g; CARB 6g; FIBER 1.5g; CHOL 99mg; IRON 1.9mg; SODIUM 465mg; CALC 35mg

INGREDIENT TIP

Tomatillos are an apple-green fruit with tangy flavor and a papery husk that splits open as the fruit matures. They're easy to find at most super-markets and add authentic Southwestern flavor to recipes.

Marinated Grilled Chicken Breast with Watermelon-Jalapeño Salsa

Sweet watermelon perfectly complements the earthy spices—oregano, chili powder, and cumin—used to marinate juicy chicken breasts.

Yield: 4 servings (serving size: 1 chicken breast half and 1 cup salsa)

1 tablespoon chopped fresh oregano

1 tablespoon extra-virgin olive oil

1 teaspoon chili powder

¾ teaspoon ground cumin

½ teaspoon salt

3 garlic cloves, minced

4 (6-ounce) skinless, boneless chicken breast halves

Cooking spray

2 cups (½-inch) cubed seeded watermelon

1 cup (½-inch) cubed peeled ripe mango

¼ cup finely chopped red onion

2 tablespoons chopped fresh cilantro

2 tablespoons finely chopped seeded jalapeño pepper (about 1 small)

1 tablespoon fresh lime juice

½ teaspoon sugar

¼ teaspoon salt

1. Combine first 6 ingredients in a large zip-top plastic bag. Add chicken to bag; seal. Marinate in refrigerator up to 4 hours, turning bag occasionally.
2. Prepare grill.
3. Place chicken on grill rack coated with cooking spray. Grill 5 minutes on each side or until done. Combine watermelon and remaining ingredients. Serve watermelon mixture with chicken.

CALORIES 304; FAT 8.3g (sat 1.8g, mono 4.1g, poly 1.4g); PROTEIN 40.7g; CARB 15.9g; FIBER 1.5g; CHOL 108mg; IRON 1.8mg; SODIUM 540mg; CALC 44mg

SAFETY TIP

When cutting or seeding jalapeño peppers, wear rubber gloves to prevent your hands from being burned. To seed the peppers, slice off the stem end, and cut the pepper in half lengthwise. Remove the seeds with a knife or

by running your finger along the inside of the vein, scraping off the seeds. Stack the two peppers halves on top of each other, and cut into irregular pieces about the size of peas.

Chicken Breasts with Tomatoes and Olives

Kalamata and picholine olives add salty flavor. Serve over couscous, with dressed greens on the side.

Yield: 4 servings

4 (6-ounce) skinless, boneless chicken breast halves

¼ teaspoon salt

¼ teaspoon freshly ground black pepper

Cooking spray

1 cup multicolored cherry or grape tomatoes, halved

3 tablespoons oil and vinegar dressing, divided

20 olives, halved

½ cup (2 ounces) crumbled feta cheese

Basil leaves, torn (optional)

1. Prepare grill to medium-high heat.

2. Sprinkle chicken evenly with ¼ teaspoon salt and ¼ teaspoon freshly ground black pepper. Place chicken on grill rack coated with cooking spray, and grill 6 minutes on each side or until chicken is done. Keep warm.

3. Combine tomatoes, 1½ tablespoons dressing, and olives in a medium skillet over medium heat, and cook 2 minutes or until tomatoes soften slightly and mixture is thoroughly heated, stirring occasionally.

4. Brush chicken with remaining 1½ tablespoons dressing. Cut each chicken breast half into ¾-inch slices. Place chicken on each of 4 plates. Top each chicken breast half with ¼ cup tomato mixture. Sprinkle each serving with 2 tablespoons cheese and torn basil leaves, if desired.

CALORIES 348; FAT 17.3g (sat 4.4g, mono 5g, poly 1.2g); PROTEIN 41.9g; CARB 3.9g; FIBER 0.6g; CHOL 111mg; IRON 1.6mg; SODIUM 810mg; CALC 100mg

Quick Barbecue Chicken

Rub chicken breasts under the skin with the spice paste, and grill for a simple, delicious late-summer dinner. Leave the skin on the chicken as it cooks so the breasts will remain juicy, and discard skin just before serving.

Yield: 2 servings (serving size: 1 chicken breast half)

1 teaspoon sugar

1 teaspoon chili powder

2 teaspoons olive oil

½ teaspoon salt

¼ teaspoon garlic powder

¼ teaspoon ground cumin

⅛ teaspoon ground ginger

⅛ teaspoon ground cinnamon

⅛ teaspoon freshly ground black pepper

2 (8-ounce) bone-in chicken breast halves

Cooking spray

1. Prepare grill.

2. Combine first 9 ingredients in a bowl, stirring well. Loosen skin from chicken by inserting fingers, gently pushing between skin and meat; rub spice mixture evenly under skin over meat. Lightly coat skin with cooking spray. Place chicken, breast-side down, on a grill rack coated with cooking spray; grill 30 minutes or until a thermometer inserted in the thickest part registers 165°, turning twice. Let chicken stand 10 minutes. Remove skin; discard.

CALORIES 308; FAT 9.7g (sat 2.1g, mono 5g, poly 1.6g); PROTEIN 49.4g; CARB 2.7g; FIBER 0.3g; CHOL 131mg; IRON 1.7mg; SODIUM 738mg; CALC 27mg

QUICK TIP

Purchase a preshredded slaw mix and bottled low-fat dressing for a quick side dish to round out this last-of-the-season grill-out menu.

Apricot-Glazed Grilled Chicken

Grilling and glazing will easily transform chicken into something special. You'll get the best results if you let the chicken stand at room temperature before grilling.

Yield: 4 servings (serving size: 1 chicken breast half or 1 thigh and 1 drumstick)

3 tablespoons apricot preserves

2 tablespoons red wine vinegar

1½ tablespoons extra-virgin olive oil

1 garlic clove, minced

2 bone-in chicken breast halves, skinned

2 bone-in chicken thighs, skinned

2 chicken drumsticks, skinned

½ teaspoon fine sea salt

¼ teaspoon freshly ground black pepper

Cooking spray

1. Combine first 4 ingredients in a small bowl, stirring well.

2. Prepare grill for indirect grilling. If using a gas grill, heat one side to medium-high and leave one side with no heat. If using a charcoal grill, arrange hot coals on one side of charcoal grate, leaving the other side empty.

3. Let chicken stand at room temperature for 30 minutes. Sprinkle chicken evenly with salt and pepper. Place chicken, meaty sides down, on grill rack coated with cooking spray over direct heat; grill 5 minutes or until browned.

4. Turn chicken over; baste with apricot mixture. Grill 5 minutes over direct heat or until browned. Turn chicken over, moving it over indirect heat; baste with apricot mixture. Cover and cook 15 minutes. Turn chicken over; baste with apricot mixture. Cook 20 minutes or until done.

CALORIES 247; FAT 10.7g (sat 2.3g, mono 5.7g, poly 1.8g); PROTEIN 26.5g; CARB 10g; FIBER 0.1g; CHOL 82mg; IRON 1.2mg; SODIUM 370mg; CALC 18mg

Marinated Grilled Chicken Legs

Here's a recipe that's sure to be a hit at your next cookout. It's quick and easy and is made with ingredients you're likely to already have on hand. For a variation, consider substituting pineapple juice for the orange juice, or lime juice for the lemon.

Yield: 4 servings (serving size: 2 drumsticks)

1 cup fresh orange juice

2 tablespoons fresh lemon juice

4 teaspoons low-sodium soy sauce

1 tablespoon dry sherry

1½ teaspoons bottled minced garlic

1½ teaspoons balsamic vinegar

1½ teaspoons basil oil

1 teaspoon onion powder

1 teaspoon dark sesame oil

½ teaspoon salt

¼ teaspoon hot pepper sauce

8 chicken drumsticks (about 2¼ pounds), skinned

Cooking spray

Green onion strips (optional)

1. Combine first 11 ingredients in a large zip-top plastic bag. Add chicken to bag; seal. Marinate in refrigerator 2 hours, turning bag occasionally.
2. Prepare grill.
3. Remove chicken from bag, reserving marinade. Place reserved marinade in a small saucepan; cook over medium heat 3 minutes. Place chicken on grill coated with cooking spray; grill 30 minutes or until chicken is done, turning and basting occasionally with reserved marinade. Garnish with green onion strips, if desired.

CALORIES 215; FAT 7.5g (sat 1.8g, mono 2.8g, poly 1.8g); PROTEIN 30g; CARB 4.4g; FIBER 0.1g; CHOL 97mg; IRON 1.5mg; SODIUM 339mg; CALC 18mg

Spiced Chicken Kebabs

Yield: 8 servings (serving size: 1 kebab and about 2 tablespoons raita)

Kebabs:

¾ cup plain low-fat yogurt

1 tablespoon grated peeled fresh ginger

2 teaspoons ground coriander

2 teaspoons paprika

1 teaspoon ground cumin

¼ teaspoon ground cardamom

¼ teaspoon ground turmeric

¼ teaspoon saffron threads, crushed

⅛ teaspoon ground cinnamon

⅛ teaspoon ground cloves

3 garlic cloves, minced

2 pounds skinless, boneless chicken thighs, cut into 1-inch chunks

1 medium red onion, cut into 1-inch chunks (about 8 ounces)

1 large red bell pepper, cut into 1-inch chunks (about 8 ounces)

1 medium zucchini, cut into 1-inch chunks (about 8 ounces)

Cooking spray

½ teaspoon salt

½ teaspoon freshly ground black pepper

Raita:

½ cup plain low-fat yogurt

⅓ cup diced seeded tomato

¼ cup cucumber, peeled, seeded, grated, and squeezed dry

¼ cup reduced-fat sour cream

1 tablespoon minced seeded jalapeño pepper

1½ teaspoons chopped fresh cilantro

¼ teaspoon ground cumin

¼ teaspoon salt

1. To prepare kebabs, combine first 12 ingredients in a large zip-top plastic bag; seal and marinate in refrigerator overnight, turning bag occasionally.
2. Prepare grill.
3. Remove chicken from bag; discard marinade. Thread chicken, onion, bell pepper, and zucchini alternately on each of 8 (12-inch) wooden skewers. Coat kebabs with cooking spray, and sprinkle with ½ teaspoon salt and black pepper. Place kebabs on grill rack coated with cooking spray. Grill 25 minutes or until chicken is done, turning occasionally. Remove from grill; keep warm.
4. To prepare raita, combine ½ cup yogurt and remaining ingredients in a small bowl. Serve with kebabs.

CALORIES 189; FAT 6g (sat 2g, mono 1.7g, poly 1.3g); PROTEIN 24.9g; CARB 8.5g; FIBER 1.7g; CHOL 99mg; IRON 1.7mg; SODIUM 344mg; CALC 81mg

INGREDIENT TIP

Saffron has always been the world's most expensive spice, but you need only a few dried stigmas to color a dish golden yellow and impart a warm, aromatic quality.

Korean Chicken with Minted Cucumbers

Here's a spin on Korean grilled chicken with a speedy kimchi-type accompaniment. We prefer using chicken thighs for this dish because they are juicier and tastier than boneless breasts. This entrée is simple enough for an after-work dinner but scrumptious enough for guests.

Yield: 4 servings

Cucumbers:

1 English cucumber, peeled, halved lengthwise, and thinly sliced (about 2½ cups)

¼ teaspoon salt

¼ cup minced shallots

2 tablespoons chopped fresh mint

1 tablespoon seasoned rice vinegar

1 tablespoon honey

1 teaspoon dark sesame oil

¼ teaspoon ground red pepper

1 serrano chile, seeded and minced

Chicken:

8 skinless, boneless chicken thighs (about 1¼ pounds)

¼ cup soy sauce

2 tablespoons dark sesame oil

1 tablespoon minced peeled fresh ginger

1 tablespoon honey

½ teaspoon freshly ground black pepper

3 garlic cloves, thinly sliced

Cooking spray

¼ cup thinly sliced green onions

4 teaspoons sesame seeds, toasted

1. To prepare cucumbers, place cucumber slices in a colander; sprinkle with salt, tossing well. Drain 1 hour. Place cucumber slices on several layers of paper towels; cover with additional paper towels. Let stand 5 minutes, pressing down occasionally. Combine cucumber, shallots, and next 6 ingredients in a large bowl; toss gently. Cover and set aside.

2. To prepare chicken, place each chicken thigh between 2 sheets of heavy-duty plastic wrap; pound to ½-inch thickness using a meat mallet or small heavy skillet. Combine soy sauce and next 5 ingredients in a large zip-top plastic bag. Add chicken to soy sauce mixture in bag; seal. Marinate in refrigerator 30 minutes, turning bag occasionally.

3. Heat a grill pan over medium-high heat. Coat pan with cooking spray. Remove chicken from bag; discard marinade. Place 4 thighs in pan; cook 6 minutes on each side or until done. Repeat procedure with remaining 4 thighs. Place 2 thighs and ½ cup cucumbers on each of 4 plates; sprinkle each serving with 1 tablespoon green onions and 1 teaspoon sesame seeds.

CALORIES 262; FAT 8.9g (sat 1.9g, mono 3g, poly 2.8g); PROTEIN 29.9g; CARB 14.9g; FIBER 1.5g; CHOL 115mg; IRON 2.7mg; SODIUM 502mg; CALC 40mg

WINE TIP

Serve an herbaceous sauvignon blanc to echo the crisp freshness of the dish's cucumber and mint.

Soy-Marinated Chicken Thighs

This good, solid recipe features a quick and easy marinade. Serve with a side of pasta and grilled pickle spears to round out your meal.

Yield: 4 servings (serving size: 2 thighs)

3 tablespoons low-sodium soy sauce

2 tablespoons extra-virgin olive oil

2 teaspoons chopped fresh thyme

8 (2-ounce) skinless, boneless chicken thighs

2 garlic cloves, minced

Cooking spray

1. Combine first 5 ingredients in a large zip-top plastic bag; seal. Marinate in refrigerator 4 hours or up to 24 hours, turning occasionally.

2. Prepare grill to medium-high heat.

3. Remove chicken from bag; discard marinade. Place chicken on grill rack coated with cooking spray; grill 3 minutes on each side or until done.

CALORIES 136; FAT 6.7g (sat 1.3g, mono 3.5g, poly 1.2g); PROTEIN 17.1g; CARB 0.8g; FIBER 0.1g; CHOL 71mg; IRON 1.1mg; SODIUM 273mg; CALC 12mg

INGREDIENT TIP

Soy sauce is great in marinades for grilled meats, as it stands up to charred flavors. Try this simple solution with steaks, pork tenderloin, or pork chops.

Barbecue Chicken with Mustard Glaze

A five-ingredient rub and a four-ingredient basting sauce are all you need to take chicken from routine to off-the-charts good. Grilled summer squash makes a light, fresh side.

Yield: 4 servings (serving size: 2 thighs)

2 tablespoons dark brown sugar

2 teaspoons garlic powder

2 teaspoons chili powder

1 teaspoon smoked paprika

½ teaspoon salt

¼ cup ketchup

1 tablespoon dark brown sugar

1 tablespoon sherry or red wine vinegar

1 tablespoon Dijon mustard

8 (6-ounce) skinless, bone-in chicken thighs

Cooking spray

1. Combine first 5 ingredients in a small bowl. Combine ketchup and next 3 ingredients in a small bowl; stir with a whisk.

2. Heat a large grill pan over medium-high heat. Rub spice mixture evenly over chicken thighs. Coat pan with cooking spray. Add chicken to pan, and cook 12 minutes. Turn chicken over. Brush with half of ketchup mixture; cook 12 minutes. Turn chicken over. Brush with remaining ketchup mixture, and cook 2 minutes or until a thermometer registers 165°.

CALORIES 226; FAT 5.5g (sat 1.4g, mono 1.7g, poly 1.4g); PROTEIN 27.7g; CARB 15.4g; FIBER 0.4g; CHOL 115mg; IRON 1.9mg; SODIUM 651mg; CALC 28mg

FLAVOR TIP

An assortment of spices mixed with common condiments makes a thick, tangy-sweet glaze with a hint of smokiness.

Grilled Chicken with Sriracha Glaze

Dense, bone-in chicken leg quarters benefit from long, slow cooking over indirect heat. The less intense heat also prevents the sweet glaze from burning. Customize the glaze according to what you have on hand; try pineapple preserves or apple jelly in place of mango jam, for example, or hot pepper sauce instead of Sriracha. Serve with a simple slaw of cabbage, carrots, lime juice, and sugar.

Yield: 4 servings (serving size: 1 leg-thigh quarter and 1 tablespoon mango mixture)

⅔ cup mango jam

2 tablespoons finely chopped fresh chives

2 tablespoons rice vinegar

2 tablespoons Sriracha (hot chile sauce, such as Huy Fong)

1 tablespoon olive oil

4 (12-ounce) bone-in chicken leg-thigh quarters, skinned

½ teaspoon kosher salt

¼ teaspoon freshly ground black pepper

1. Prepare grill for indirect grilling. If using a gas grill, heat one side to medium-high and leave one side with no heat. If using a charcoal grill, arrange hot coals on either side of charcoal grate, leaving an empty space in the middle.
2. Combine mango jam, chives, vinegar, and Sriracha, stirring until smooth. Reserve ¼ cup mango mixture; set aside.
3. Brush oil evenly over chicken. Sprinkle chicken with salt and pepper.
4. Carefully remove grill rack. Place a disposable aluminum foil pan on unheated part of grill. Carefully return grill rack to grill. Place chicken on grill rack over unheated part. Brush chicken with about 2 tablespoons remaining mango mixture. Close lid; grill 90 minutes or until a thermometer inserted into meaty part of thigh registers 165°, turning chicken and brushing with about 2 tablespoons mango mixture every 20 minutes. Transfer the chicken to a platter. Drizzle chicken with reserved ¼ cup mango mixture.

CALORIES 326; FAT 10.4g (sat 2.3g, mono 4.7g, poly 2.1g); PROTEIN 38.7g; CARB 18.2g; FIBER 2.7g; CHOL 154mg; IRON 4.5mg; SODIUM 515mg; CALC 102mg

INGREDIENT TIP

Sriracha is a moderately hot and spicy chili sauce that's reminiscent of barbecue sauce. The most common brand, Huy Fong, comes in a clear plastic squeeze bottle with a rooster on the label and a bright green cap.

Lemon Tarragon-Brined Whole Chicken

This chicken is best when cooked indirectly on a grill, but you can also roast it in an oven. Toss any leftover chicken with tarragon-flavored mayonnaise for a salad.

Yield: 5 servings (serving size: about 4 ounces)

7 cups water, divided

2 tablespoons grated lemon rind

8 fresh tarragon sprigs

1 cup kosher salt (such as Diamond Crystal)

½ cup sugar

2 cups ice cubes

1 (4½-pound) roasting chicken

1 tablespoon chopped fresh tarragon, divided

2 teaspoons freshly ground black pepper, divided

Cooking spray

¼ cup fresh lemon juice, divided

1. Combine 1 cup water, rind, and tarragon sprigs in a small saucepan. Bring to a boil; remove from heat. Place in a large bowl; cool to room temperature. Add remaining 6 cups water, salt, and sugar, stirring until salt and sugar dissolve. Place salt mixture in a 2-gallon zip-top plastic bag. Add ice and chicken; seal. Refrigerate 3 hours, turning bag occasionally. Remove chicken from bag; discard brine. Pat chicken dry with paper towels.

2. Prepare grill for indirect grilling. If using a gas grill, heat one side to medium and leave one side with no heat. If using a charcoal grill, arrange hot coals on either side of charcoal grate, leaving an empty space in the middle.

3. Sprinkle cavity of chicken with 1½ teaspoons chopped tarragon and 1 teaspoon pepper. Lightly coat outside of chicken with cooking spray. Rub remaining 1½ teaspoons chopped tarragon and 1 teaspoon pepper evenly over outside of chicken. Place chicken on grill rack coated with cooking spray over unheated side. Close lid; grill 15 minutes. Brush chicken with 2 table-spoons lemon juice. Close lid; grill an additional 30 minutes. Brush with remaining lemon juice. Close lid; grill 15 minutes or until thermometer inserted into meaty part of thigh registers 180°.

4. Place chicken on a platter; cover with foil. Let stand 15 minutes. Discard skin.

CALORIES 246; FAT 8.4g (sat 2.3g, mono 3.1g, poly 1.9g); PROTEIN 37g; CARB 3.3g; FIBER 0.1g; CHOL 109mg; IRON 1.8mg; SODIUM 1505mg; CALC 29mg

INGREDIENT TIP

Fresh tarragon has a brighter flavor than dried, but you can use a third the amount of dried if fresh is unavailable.

Grilled Spice-Rubbed Whole Chicken

This chicken is sure to turn out juicy and flavorful. For even more flavor, consider increasing the amount of the rub and add it to the legs and thighs.

Yield: 4 servings (serving size: 1 chicken breast half or 1 thigh and 1 drumstick)

1½ teaspoons brown sugar

1¼ teaspoons ground cumin

1 teaspoon kosher salt

½ teaspoon freshly ground black pepper

½ teaspoon paprika

½ teaspoon dried thyme

½ teaspoon chili powder

1 (4-pound) whole chicken

Cooking spray

1. Prepare grill for indirect grilling. If using a gas grill, heat one side to medium-high and leave one side with no heat. If using a charcoal grill, arrange hot coals on either side of charcoal grate, leaving an empty space in the middle.

2. Combine first 7 ingredients; set aside.

3. Remove and discard giblets and neck from chicken. Trim excess fat. Place chicken, breast side down, on a cutting surface. Cut chicken in half lengthwise along backbone, cutting to, but not through, other side. Turn chicken over. Starting at neck cavity, loosen skin from breast and drumsticks by inserting fingers, gently pushing between skin and meat. Rub spice mixture under skin. Gently press skin to secure.

4. Place chicken, breast side down, on grill rack coated with cooking spray over direct heat; cover and cook 7 minutes. Turn chicken over; cook 7 minutes. Move chicken over indirect heat; cover and cook 45 minutes or until a thermometer inserted in meaty part of thigh registers 165°. Transfer chicken to a cutting board; let rest 10 minutes. Discard skin.

CALORIES 270; FAT 6.5g (sat 1.6g, mono 1.9g, poly 1.6g); PROTEIN 47.3g; CARB 2.6g; FIBER 0.6g; CHOL 150mg; IRON 2.8mg; SODIUM 657mg; CALC 40mg

stovetop
suppers

Chicken, Mushroom, and Gruyère Quesadillas

Build on the traditional Mexican classic by adding fun new ingredients like sliced mushrooms and a different creamy cheese. Watermelon-jicama salad is a refreshing side for this easy summer dish. Combine 4 cups (½-inch) cubed seedless watermelon, 1½ cups (½-inch) cubed peeled jicama, 1 cup chopped English cucumber, and ½ cup chopped red onion. Add 2 table-spoons fresh lemon juice, 2 teaspoons sugar, and 1 teaspoon olive oil; toss well.

Yield: 4 servings (serving size: ½ quesadilla)

1 teaspoon olive oil

1 cup presliced mushrooms

½ cup thinly sliced onion

⅛ teaspoon salt

⅛ teaspoon freshly ground black pepper

1 teaspoon bottled minced garlic

1 tablespoon sherry or red wine vinegar

2 (10-inch) fat-free flour tortillas

1 cup shredded cooked chicken breast (about 8 ounces)

1 cup arugula

½ cup (2 ounces) shredded Gruyère cheese

Cooking spray

1. Heat a large nonstick skillet over medium-high heat. Add olive oil to pan; swirl to coat. Add mushrooms, sliced onion, salt, and pepper to pan; sauté 5 minutes. Stir in garlic, and sauté 30 seconds. Add vinegar; cook 30 seconds or until liquid almost evaporates.

2. Arrange half of mushroom mixture over half of each tortilla. Top each tortilla with ½ cup chicken, ½ cup arugula, and ¼ cup cheese; fold tortillas in half.

3. Wipe pan clean with a paper towel. Heat pan over medium heat. Coat pan with cooking spray. Add tortillas to pan. Place a heavy skillet on top of tortillas; cook 2 minutes on each side or until crisp.

CALORIES 270; FAT 8.9g (sat 3.7g, mono 3g, poly 0.8g); PROTEIN 25.2g; CARB 20.3g; FIBER 3g; CHOL 64mg; IRON 1.7mg; SODIUM 391mg; CALC 242mg

INGREDIENT TIP

Use baby spinach in place of arugula, if you like.

Chicken Strips with Blue Cheese Dressing

Pair this fiery entrée with cool, crunchy carrot and celery sticks.

Yield: 4 servings (serving size: about 3 chicken tenders and 2 tablespoons dressing)

Chicken:

½ cup low-fat buttermilk

½ teaspoon hot sauce

2.25 ounces all-purpose flour (about ½ cup)

½ teaspoon paprika

½ teaspoon ground red pepper

½ teaspoon freshly ground black pepper

¼ teaspoon salt

1 pound chicken breast tenders

1 tablespoon canola oil

Dressing:

½ cup fat-free mayonnaise

¼ cup (1 ounce) crumbled blue cheese

1 tablespoon red wine vinegar

1 teaspoon bottled minced garlic

¼ teaspoon salt

¼ teaspoon freshly ground black pepper

1. To prepare chicken, combine buttermilk and hot sauce in a shallow dish. Combine flour and next 4 ingredients in a shallow dish. Dip chicken in buttermilk mixture, and dredge chicken in flour mixture.

2. Heat oil in a large nonstick skillet over medium-high heat. Add chicken; cook 4 minutes on each side or until done. Remove from pan. Set aside, and keep warm.

3. While chicken cooks, prepare the dressing. Combine fat-free mayonnaise and remaining ingredients in a small bowl. Serve with chicken strips.

CALORIES 281; FAT 8.7g (sat 2.6g, mono 3.2g, poly 1.5g); PROTEIN 30.8g; CARB 18.4g; FIBER 1.3g; CHOL 77mg; IRON 1.9mg; SODIUM 771mg; CALC 101mg

Thai Chicken Sauté

Use less hot sauce for milder flavor.

Yield: 4 servings (serving size: 1½ cups chicken mixture, ½ cup rice, and 1 lime wedge)

1 (3½-ounce) bag boil-in-bag rice

1½ pounds chicken breast tenders

1 tablespoon cornstarch

1 tablespoon fish sauce

4 teaspoons canola oil, divided

1 cup sliced onion

2 teaspoons bottled minced garlic

1 teaspoon bottled ground fresh
ginger (such as Spice World)

½ cup light coconut milk

2 tablespoons Sriracha (hot chile
sauce, such as Huy Fong)

1 tablespoon sugar

1 tablespoon fresh lime juice

4 lime wedges

2 tablespoons chopped fresh
cilantro

1. Cook rice according to package directions, omitting salt and fat.
Keep warm.
2. Toss chicken with cornstarch and fish sauce. Heat 1 tablespoon oil in a
large nonstick skillet over medium-high heat. Add chicken to pan; sauté
5 minutes. Remove chicken from pan. Heat remaining 1 teaspoon oil in pan.
Add onion, garlic, and ginger to pan; sauté 1 minute. Return chicken to pan;
cook 1 minute or until done. Stir in coconut milk, Sriracha, sugar, and juice;
cook 45 seconds or until thoroughly heated. Serve chicken mixture over rice
with lime wedges. Sprinkle each serving with 1½ teaspoons cilantro.

CALORIES 403; FAT 10.8g (sat 3.1g, mono 4.3g, poly 2.4g); PROTEIN 42.6g; CARB 31.4g; FIBER 0.5g;
CHOL 108mg; IRON 2.4mg; SODIUM 650mg; CALC 32mg

Sesame Chicken Edamame Bowl

The slightly sweet and nutty stir-fried vegetables complement the delicately flavored chicken. You can serve this over udon noodles or rice stick noodles instead of rice.

Yield: 6 servings (serving size: ⅔ cup chicken mixture and ⅓ cup rice)

2 teaspoons canola oil

1 tablespoon minced peeled fresh ginger

2 teaspoons minced peeled fresh lemongrass

2 garlic cloves, minced

1 pound skinless, boneless chicken breast, cut into bite-sized pieces

2 cups frozen shelled edamame (green soybeans)

2 cups frozen bell pepper stir-fry mix

2 tablespoons low-sodium soy sauce

1 tablespoon mirin (sweet rice wine)

1 teaspoon dark sesame oil

¼ teaspoon cornstarch

½ cup (¼-inch) diagonally cut green onions

2 teaspoons dark sesame seeds

½ teaspoon salt

2 cups hot cooked brown rice

1. Heat canola oil in a large nonstick skillet over medium-high heat. Add ginger, lemongrass, and garlic; sauté 1 minute or just until mixture begins to brown. Add chicken; sauté 2 minutes. Add edamame and stir-fry mix; sauté 3 minutes. Combine soy sauce, mirin, sesame oil, and cornstarch, stirring with a whisk. Add to pan; cook 1 minute. Remove from heat. Stir in onions, sesame seeds, and salt. Serve over rice.

CALORIES 277; FAT 6.5g (sat 0.7g, mono 2.3g, poly 2.6g); PROTEIN 25.5g; CARB 27.1g; FIBER 5.4g; CHOL 44mg; IRON 2.4mg; SODIUM 452mg; CALC 72mg

QUICK TIP

Some frozen foods perform well even without thawing, including berries and bell pepper stir-fry mixes. The same holds true for frozen shelled edamame. You can also save prep time when thawing isn't required.

Sweet and Sour Chicken

Serve this beloved traditional favorite over long-grain white rice for a complete, well-balanced meal.

Yield: 4 servings (serving size: about 1 cup)

1 tablespoon olive oil

1 tablespoon bottled minced garlic

1 teaspoon bottled ground fresh ginger (such as Spice World)

¼ teaspoon crushed red pepper

1½ pounds skinless, boneless chicken breast, cut into ½-inch pieces

¾ cup chopped onion

½ cup chopped celery

½ cup chopped red bell pepper

1 (15¼-ounce) can pineapple chunks in juice, undrained

⅓ cup reduced-sodium soy sauce

2 tablespoons dry sherry

1½ tablespoons cornstarch

2 teaspoons brown sugar

¼ cup dry-roasted chopped cashews

1. Heat oil in a large nonstick skillet over medium-high heat. Add garlic, ginger, red pepper, and chicken to pan; sauté 5 minutes or until chicken is done. Remove chicken mixture from pan; set aside.

2. Add onion, celery, and bell pepper to pan, and sauté 4 minutes or until crisp-tender. Drain pineapple, reserving ½ cup juice. Add 1 cup pineapple chunks to pan; cook 30 seconds. Reserve remaining pineapple for another use. Combine reserved ½ cup juice, soy sauce, sherry, cornstarch, and sugar in a bowl, stirring with a whisk until smooth.

3. Return chicken mixture to pan. Stir in juice mixture; bring to boil. Cook 1 minute. Sprinkle with cashews.

CALORIES 388; FAT 11.6g (sat 2.4g, mono 6.2g, poly 2g); PROTEIN 41.5g; CARB 28.9g; FIBER 2.1g; CHOL 101mg; IRON 2.7mg; SODIUM 858mg; CALC 58mg

QUICK TIP

To save time, cut the chicken into pieces while you wait for the pan to heat.

Fiesta Chicken Tacos with Mango and Jicama Salad

Try this with a side of chipotle *refritos*. Combine 1 tablespoon fresh lime juice, 1 teaspoon minced canned chipotle chile in adobo sauce, 1 (16-ounce) can refried beans, and 1 minced garlic clove in a saucepan. Cook over medium heat 5 minutes or until thoroughly heated. Sprinkle with 2 teaspoons chopped fresh cilantro.

Yield: 4 servings (serving size: 2 tacos)

Salad:

¾ cup (3-inch) julienne-cut peeled jicama

½ cup sliced peeled ripe mango

¼ cup presliced red onion

1 tablespoon fresh lime juice

½ teaspoon sugar

1½ teaspoons chopped fresh cilantro

¼ teaspoon salt

Dash of black pepper

Tacos:

1 tablespoon olive oil, divided

1 pound skinless, boneless chicken breast, cut into thin strips

½ teaspoon chili powder

½ teaspoon ground cumin

⅛ teaspoon ground chipotle chile pepper

1 cup presliced red bell pepper

1 cup presliced red onion

¼ teaspoon salt

8 (6-inch) corn tortillas

1 cup mixed salad greens

1. To prepare salad, combine first 8 ingredients.

2. To prepare tacos, heat 2 teaspoons oil in a large nonstick skillet over medium-high heat. Sprinkle chicken evenly with chili powder, cumin, and chipotle pepper. Add chicken mixture to pan; sauté 3 minutes. Remove from pan.

3. Heat remaining 1 teaspoon oil in pan. Add bell pepper and 1 cup onion; cook 3 minutes or until crisp-tender. Return chicken mixture to pan; cook 2 minutes or until chicken is done. Sprinkle with ¼ teaspoon salt.

4. Heat tortillas according to package directions. Arrange 2 tablespoons mixed greens, about ⅓ cup chicken mixture, and about 2 tablespoons salad in each tortilla; fold over.

CALORIES 320; FAT 6.4g (sat 1.1g, mono 3.2g, poly 1.3g); PROTEIN 30.4g; CARB 36.1g; FIBER 5.8g; CHOL 66mg; IRON 2.2mg; SODIUM 471mg; CALC 129mg

INGREDIENT TIP

Find jicama year-round in the produce section of many supermarkets and Latin American markets. Select firm, dry jicama roots. Skin should not appear shriveled, bruised, or blemished.

Chicken Puttanesca with Angel Hair Pasta

Delicious, easy, and quick—you couldn't ask for more for a weeknight meal. Round it out with a tossed green salad and dinner is done.

Yield: 4 servings

8 ounces uncooked angel hair pasta

2 teaspoons olive oil

4 (6-ounce) skinless, boneless chicken breast halves

½ teaspoon salt

2 cups tomato-basil pasta sauce (such as Muir Glen Organic)

¼ cup pitted and coarsely chopped kalamata olives

1 tablespoon capers

¼ teaspoon crushed red pepper

¼ cup (1 ounce) preshredded Parmesan cheese

Thinly sliced fresh basil or basil sprigs (optional)

1. Cook pasta according to package directions, omitting salt and fat. Drain and keep warm.

2. Heat oil in a large nonstick skillet over medium-high heat. Cut chicken into 1-inch pieces. Add chicken to pan; sprinkle evenly with salt. Cook chicken 5 minutes or until lightly browned, stirring occasionally. Stir in pasta sauce, olives, capers, and pepper; bring to a simmer. Cook 5 minutes or until chicken is done, stirring frequently. Arrange 1 cup pasta on each of 4 plates; top with 1½ cups chicken mixture. Sprinkle each serving with 1 tablespoon cheese. Garnish with sliced basil or basil sprigs, if desired.

CALORIES 530; FAT 12.4g (sat 2.8g, mono 6.6g, poly 2g); PROTEIN 51.8g; CARB 55g; FIBER 2.1g; CHOL 104mg; IRON 4.2mg; SODIUM 971mg; CALC 165mg

FLAVOR TIP

We add olives, capers, and crushed red pepper to bottled pasta sauce for a quick variation on the traditional version.

Chicken Scaloppine with Broccoli Rabe

If you can't find cutlets, place chicken breast halves between two sheets of heavy-duty plastic wrap, and pound to ¼-inch thickness using a meat mallet. Broccoli florets can be substituted for broccoli rabe; the cooking time may be a little longer, though. Add a side of roasted potato wedges and carrots, if desired.

Yield: 4 servings (serving size: 1 cutlet and ½ cup broccoli rabe mixture)

1 tablespoon olive oil

⅓ cup Italian-seasoned breadcrumbs

¼ teaspoon black pepper

4 (6-ounce) skinless, boneless chicken breast cutlets

½ cup dry white wine

½ cup fat-free, less-sodium chicken broth

3 tablespoons fresh lemon juice

1 teaspoon butter

1 pound broccoli rabe (rapini), cut into 3-inch pieces

2 tablespoons chopped fresh parsley

2 tablespoons capers, rinsed and drained

4 lemon slices (optional)

Parsley sprigs (optional)

1. Heat oil in a large nonstick skillet over medium-high heat.

2. Combine breadcrumbs and pepper in a shallow dish; dredge chicken in breadcrumb mixture. Add chicken to pan; cook 3 minutes on each side or until done. Remove from pan; keep warm.

3. Add wine, broth, juice, and butter to pan, scraping pan to loosen browned bits. Stir in broccoli rabe; cover and cook 3 minutes or until broccoli rabe is tender. Stir in chopped parsley and capers. Serve chicken over broccoli rabe mixture. Garnish with lemon slices and parsley sprigs, if desired.

CALORIES 318; FAT 7.4g (sat 1.7g, mono 3.3g, poly 1g); PROTEIN 44.3g; CARB 14g; FIBER 3.9g; CHOL 101mg; IRON 2.9mg; SODIUM 577mg; CALC 102mg

Skillet Chicken Breast Aglio e Olio

Chicken benefits from the strong flavors of garlic, capers, and cherry peppers in the sauce for this dish. You can use more or fewer capers to suit your taste. Sample the sauce before serving to be sure the flavors are balanced. Breadcrumbs serve as a thickener, lending the sauce body and texture. Serve with green beans and rice.

Yield: 6 servings (serving size: 1 chicken breast half and about 2½ tablespoons sauce)

6 (6-ounce) skinless, boneless chicken breast halves

½ teaspoon salt, divided

1.5 ounces all-purpose flour (about ⅓ cup)

1 tablespoon olive oil

2 tablespoons butter

8 garlic cloves, thinly sliced

2 to 3 tablespoons capers, drained

4 pickled hot cherry peppers, halved and seeded

1 cup organic vegetable broth (such as Swanson Certified Organic)

1 tablespoon dry breadcrumbs

3 tablespoons chopped fresh flat-leaf parsley

1. Sprinkle chicken with ¼ teaspoon salt. Dredge chicken in flour.

2. Heat oil and butter in a large nonstick skillet over medium heat. Add chicken; cook 4 minutes on each side or until browned. Add garlic; cook 30 seconds. Add capers and peppers; cook 30 seconds. Add broth; bring to a boil. Reduce heat, and simmer 5 minutes or until chicken is done. Stir in breadcrumbs; cook until liquid thickens (about 1 minute). Taste sauce, and add remaining ¼ teaspoon salt, if needed. Remove from heat; sprinkle with parsley.

CALORIES 286; FAT 8.5g (sat 3.3g, mono 3.3g, poly 0.9g); PROTEIN 40.9g; CARB 9.1g; FIBER 0.6g; CHOL 109mg; IRON 2mg; SODIUM 831mg; CALC 42mg

Chicken with Provençal Sauce

Capturing every morsel of chicken flavor is the secret to this quick-to-prepare dinner favorite. The tiny browned bits that remain in the skillet after the chicken is cooked are key. Serve with roasted potato wedges.

Yield: 4 servings (serving size: 1 chicken breast half and about 2 tablespoons sauce)

4 (6-ounce) skinless, boneless chicken breast halves

¼ teaspoon salt

¼ teaspoon freshly ground black pepper

1½ tablespoons olive oil

1 garlic clove, minced

1 cup fat-free, less-sodium chicken broth

1½ teaspoons dried herbes de Provence

1 teaspoon butter

1 teaspoon fresh lemon juice

Thyme sprigs (optional)

1. Place each chicken breast half between 2 sheets of heavy-duty plastic wrap; pound to ½-inch thickness using a meat mallet or rolling pin. Sprinkle chicken evenly with salt and pepper.

2. Heat oil in a large nonstick skillet over medium heat. Add chicken; cook 6 minutes on each side or until done. Remove chicken from pan; keep warm.

3. Add garlic to pan; cook 1 minute, stirring constantly. Add broth and herbes de Provence; bring to a boil, scraping pan to loosen browned bits. Cook until broth mixture is reduced to ½ cup (about 3 minutes). Remove from heat; add butter and lemon juice, stirring until butter melts. Serve sauce over chicken. Garnish with thyme sprigs, if desired.

CALORIES 248; FAT 8.2g (sat 1.8g, mono 4.5g, poly 1g); PROTEIN 40.2g; CARB 1g; FIBER 0.3g; CHOL 101mg; IRON 1.5mg; SODIUM 376mg; CALC 32mg

INGREDIENT TIP

With a heady combination of dried basil, thyme, marjoram, rosemary, lavender, and sage, herbes de Provence is a classic French seasoning. Try it in other Mediterranean dishes, such as pasta sauce or baked black olives.

Chicken Breasts with Tomatillo Salsa and Queso Fresco

Moist, well-seasoned chicken is topped with fantastically flavorful tomatillo salsa and queso fresco. If you're short on time you can use a bottled salsa verde, but we think this fresh salsa may be the best-tasting salsa you'll find.

Yield: 4 servings (serving size: 1 chicken breast half, ¼ cup salsa, and 2 tablespoons cheese)

Salsa:

2 quarts water

½ pound tomatillos (about 10 small), husks and stems removed

1 garlic clove

½ to 1 serrano chile

½ cup chopped fresh cilantro

¼ cup coarsely chopped onion

1 teaspoon fresh lime juice

¼ teaspoon salt

Chicken:

3 (1-ounce) slices white bread

4 (6-ounce) skinless, boneless chicken breast halves

½ teaspoon salt

½ teaspoon ground cumin

¼ teaspoon ground red pepper

1 large egg, lightly beaten

1 tablespoon olive oil

½ cup (2 ounces) crumbled queso fresco cheese

Cilantro sprigs (optional)

Lime wedges (optional)

1. Preheat oven to 350°.

2. To prepare salsa, bring water to a boil. Add tomatillos, garlic, and chile; cook 7 minutes. Drain and rinse with cold water. Place tomatillos, garlic, chile, chopped cilantro, onion, lime juice, and ¼ teaspoon salt in a food processor or blender; pulse 4 to 5 times or until coarsely chopped. Set aside.

3. To prepare chicken, place bread in a food processor, and pulse 10 times or until coarse crumbs measure 1½ cups. Arrange crumbs on a baking sheet; bake at 350° for 3 minutes or until lightly browned. Cool completely.

4. Place each chicken breast half between 2 sheets of heavy-duty plastic wrap; pound to ½-inch thickness using a meat mallet or rolling pin. Combine ½ teaspoon salt, cumin, and red pepper; sprinkle evenly over chicken.

5. Place breadcrumbs in a shallow dish. Place egg in another shallow dish. Dip chicken in egg; dredge in breadcrumbs.

6. Heat oil in a large nonstick skillet over medium-high heat. Add chicken; cook 4 minutes on each side or until done. Top chicken with salsa, and sprinkle with queso fresco cheese. Garnish with cilantro sprigs and lime wedges, if desired.

CALORIES 364; FAT 10.7g (sat 3.2g, mono 4.5g, poly 1.6g); PROTEIN 47.1g; CARB 17.7g; FIBER 2g; CHOL 162mg; IRON 3mg; SODIUM 770mg; CALC 169mg

INGREDIENT TIP

Queso fresco is a Mexican cheese that is mild, crumbly, and a bit salty. It's a wonderful topping for the tangy tomatillo salsa.

Sesame-Orange Chicken

Ground sesame seeds thicken the sauce as it cooks. Serve with a salad and bread.

Yield: 4 servings (serving size: 1 chicken breast half and 3 tablespoons sauce)

2 tablespoons sesame seeds, toasted

1 tablespoon grated orange rind

¼ teaspoon salt, divided

Dash of ground red pepper

4 (6-ounce) skinless, boneless chicken breast halves

2 teaspoons canola oil

1 teaspoon butter

1 cup fat-free, less-sodium chicken broth

⅓ cup orange juice

1 tablespoon whipping cream

1. Place sesame seeds, rind, ⅛ teaspoon salt, and pepper in a food processor; process until mixture resembles coarse meal.

2. Place each chicken breast half between 2 sheets of heavy-duty plastic wrap; pound to ¼-inch thickness using a meat mallet or rolling pin. Sprinkle chicken evenly with ⅛ teaspoon salt.

3. Heat oil and butter in a large nonstick skillet over medium heat until butter melts. Add chicken; cook 6 minutes on each side or until done. Remove chicken from pan; keep warm.

4. Add ground sesame mixture to pan, stirring with a whisk. Add broth, and bring to a boil, scraping pan to loosen browned bits. Cook broth mixture until reduced to ⅔ cup (about 3 minutes). Add orange juice and cream; cook 30 seconds, stirring constantly. Serve sauce over chicken.

CALORIES 271; FAT 9.1g (sat 2.5g, mono 3.4g, poly 2.2g); PROTEIN 41.1g; CARB 4g; FIBER 0.7g; CHOL 106mg; IRON 1.9mg; SODIUM 377mg; CALC 70mg

QUICK TIP

Pounding chicken breast halves cuts the cooking time in half while leaving the chicken moist and tender. To easily pound a chicken breast, place each breast between two sheets of heavy-duty plastic wrap; pound to desired thickness— usually ¼- to ½-inch thick—using a meat mallet or rolling pin.

Moroccan Chicken with Fruit and Olive Topping

The pairing of dried fruit and olives is also characteristic of other North African cuisines, such as Tunisian and Algerian. Serve over Israeli couscous, a pearl-like pasta; sprinkle with chopped green onions.

Yield: 4 servings (serving size: 1 chicken breast half and about ⅓ cup fruit mixture)

1 tablespoon olive oil, divided

½ teaspoon salt

¼ teaspoon black pepper

¼ teaspoon dried thyme

4 (6-ounce) skinless, boneless chicken breasts

½ cup prechopped onion

2 teaspoons bottled minced garlic

¾ cup dried mixed fruit

½ cup dry white wine

½ cup fat-free, less-sodium chicken broth

¼ cup chopped pitted green olives

⅛ teaspoon salt

⅛ teaspoon black pepper

1. Heat 2 teaspoons oil in a large nonstick skillet over medium-high heat. Sprinkle ½ teaspoon salt, ¼ teaspoon pepper, and thyme evenly over chicken. Add chicken to pan; cook 4 minutes on each side or until done. Remove from pan; cover and keep warm.

2. Heat remaining 1 teaspoon oil in pan. Add onion to pan; sauté 2 minutes until tender. Add garlic to pan; sauté 30 seconds. Add fruit and remaining ingredients to pan; cook 5 minutes or until liquid almost evaporates. Serve over chicken.

CALORIES 346; FAT 7.5g (sat 1g, mono 4.3g, poly 1.3g); PROTEIN 40.6g; CARB 26g; FIBER 2.1g; CHOL 99mg; IRON 2.4mg; SODIUM 591mg; CALC 45mg

INGREDIENT TIP

Pearl-like Israeli couscous, also known as maftoul, has larger-sized grains than regular couscous and takes on the consistency of macaroni when prepared. It cooks longer than regular couscous due to its size, but its size allows it to absorb plenty of liquid and flavor. Look for it in specialty and Middle Eastern markets.

Chicken with Dried Plums and Sage

Add quick-cooking whole wheat couscous and steamed green beans.

Yield: 4 servings (serving size: 1 chicken breast half and about ½ cup sauce)

4 (6-ounce) skinless, boneless chicken breast halves

2 tablespoons chopped fresh sage, divided

½ teaspoon salt

¼ teaspoon black pepper, divided

4 teaspoons olive oil, divided

2 cups thinly sliced onion (about 1 large)

½ cup dry white wine

½ cup fat-free, less-sodium chicken broth

12 pitted dried plums, halved

1½ teaspoons balsamic vinegar

1. Place each chicken breast half between 2 sheets of heavy-duty plastic wrap; pound to ½-inch thickness using a meat mallet or small heavy skillet. Sprinkle chicken with 1 tablespoon sage, salt, and ⅛ teaspoon pepper.

2. Heat 2 teaspoons oil in a large nonstick skillet over medium heat. Add chicken to pan; cook 3 minutes on each side or until done. Remove chicken from pan; keep warm. Heat remaining 2 teaspoons oil in pan. Add onion to pan; cook 3 minutes or until tender. Stir in wine and broth; bring to a boil. Add remaining 1 tablespoon sage and dried plums to pan; cook 4 minutes or until mixture thickens. Stir in remaining ⅛ teaspoon pepper and vinegar. Serve with chicken.

CALORIES 301; FAT 8.7g (sat 1.8g, mono 4.7g, poly 1.4g); PROTEIN 35.4g; CARB 19.8g; FIBER 2.3g; CHOL 94mg; IRON 1.6mg; SODIUM 438mg; CALC 49mg

Ginger-Garlic Chicken with Fresh Fig Pan Sauce

Serve over jasmine rice to soak up the savory sauce. Grill baby bok choy and carrots for a quick side dish.

Yield: 4 servings (serving size: 1 chicken breast half and about ⅓ cup sauce)

4 (6-ounce) skinless, boneless chicken breast halves

1 teaspoon grated peeled fresh ginger

¾ teaspoon kosher salt, divided

1 large garlic clove, grated

1 tablespoon canola oil

2 tablespoons thinly sliced green onion bottoms

1 pound ripe Kadota or Brown Turkey figs, cut into ¼-inch-thick wedges

2 tablespoons rice vinegar

1 teaspoon dark sesame oil

2 tablespoons thinly sliced green onion tops

½ teaspoon sesame seeds, toasted

1. Place each chicken breast half between 2 sheets of heavy-duty plastic wrap; pound each chicken breast half to ¼-inch thickness using a meat mallet or small heavy skillet.

2. Combine ginger, ½ teaspoon salt, and garlic in a small bowl; mash with a spoon to form a paste. Rub paste evenly over chicken; cover and chill 20 minutes. Heat a large nonstick skillet over medium-high heat. Add oil to pan; swirl to coat. Add chicken to pan; cook 2 minutes on each side or until done. Remove chicken from pan; keep warm. Add green onion bottoms to pan; sauté 1 minute, stirring frequently. Add figs; sauté 2 minutes, stirring frequently. Stir in remaining ¼ teaspoon salt, vinegar, and sesame oil. Remove from heat; spoon sauce over chicken. Sprinkle with green onion tops and sesame seeds.

CALORIES 318; FAT 7.3g (sat 1.1g, mono 3.2g, poly 2.2g); PROTEIN 40.4g; CARB 22.7g; FIBER 3.5g; CHOL 99mg; IRON 1.8mg; SODIUM 466mg; CALC 65mg

INGREDIENT TIP

Fresh figs are available twice a year: The first crop is available from June through July; the second crop begins early in September and lasts through mid-October. The figs from the first crop are larger and more flavorful than those from the second. Figs are extremely perishable, so you should use them soon after they're purchased, or store them in the refrigerator for no more than 2 to 3 days.

Cilantro-Lime Chicken with Avocado Salsa

Here's a terrific recipe for a busy weeknight or for a casual alfresco dinner party. It's especially wonderful in the summer since it's so simple and flavorful. Serve with saffron rice to round out the meal.

Yield: 4 servings (serving size: 1 chicken breast half and about ¼ cup salsa)

Chicken:

2 tablespoons minced fresh cilantro

2½ tablespoons fresh lime juice

1½ tablespoons olive oil

4 (6-ounce) skinless, boneless chicken breast halves

¼ teaspoon salt

Cooking spray

Salsa:

1 cup chopped plum tomato (about 2)

2 tablespoons finely chopped onion

2 teaspoons fresh lime juice

¼ teaspoon salt

⅛ teaspoon freshly ground black pepper

1 avocado, peeled and finely chopped

1. To prepare chicken, combine first 4 ingredients in a large bowl; toss and let stand 3 minutes. Remove chicken from marinade; discard marinade. Sprinkle chicken evenly with ¼ teaspoon salt. Heat a grill pan over medium-high heat. Coat pan with cooking spray. Add chicken to pan; cook 6 minutes on each side or until done.

2. To prepare salsa, combine tomato and next 4 ingredients in a medium bowl. Add avocado; stir gently to combine. Serve salsa over chicken.

CALORIES 289; FAT 13.2g (sat 2.4g, mono 7.5g, poly 1.9g); PROTEIN 35.6g; CARB 6.6g; FIBER 3.6g; CHOL 94mg; IRON 1.6mg; SODIUM 383mg; CALC 29mg

FLAVOR TIP

A three-minute dip into a pungent marinade is all that's needed to deliver big flavor to these chicken breasts. In addition, just-squeezed citrus brightens the taste of the chicken and adds zip to the simple toss-together salsa.

Parmesan Chicken Paillards with Cherry Tomato Sauce

Paillards are boneless, skinless chicken breasts pounded flat and sautéed. A crust of Parmesan adds flavor. The savory marinara sauce features the freshness of cherry tomatoes. Serve with green beans and orzo with parsley.

Yield: 4 servings (serving size: 1 chicken breast half and about ⅓ cup tomato mixture)

4 (6-ounce) skinless, boneless chicken breast halves

½ teaspoon kosher salt, divided

½ teaspoon freshly ground black pepper, divided

¼ cup grated Parmesan cheese

1 tablespoon all-purpose flour

2 teaspoons olive oil, divided

Cooking spray

½ cup finely chopped onion

¼ cup fat-free, less-sodium chicken broth

1 tablespoon sherry vinegar

2 cups quartered cherry tomatoes

½ teaspoon dried oregano

1. Place each chicken breast half between 2 sheets of heavy-duty plastic wrap; pound to ½-inch thickness using a meat mallet or small heavy skillet. Sprinkle chicken with ¼ teaspoon salt and ¼ teaspoon pepper. Combine cheese and flour in a shallow dish. Dredge 1 side of each chicken breast half in cheese mixture.

2. Heat 1 teaspoon oil in a large nonstick skillet over medium-high heat. Add 2 chicken breast halves, cheese side down; cook 4 minutes on each side or until done. Repeat procedure with remaining 1 teaspoon oil and chicken breast halves. Remove from pan; keep warm.

3. Coat pan with cooking spray. Add onion; sauté 2 minutes. Stir in broth and vinegar; cook 1 minute or until liquid almost evaporates. Add tomatoes, remaining ¼ teaspoon salt, remaining ¼ teaspoon pepper, and oregano; cook 2 minutes. Serve with chicken.

CALORIES 264; FAT 5.9g (sat 1.8g, mono 2.6g, poly 0.9g); PROTEIN 42.6g; CARB 7.4g; FIBER 1.3g; CHOL 102mg; IRON 1.6mg; SODIUM 504mg; CALC 95mg

WINE TIP

These chicken breasts have a piquant Italian flavor. Serve them with an Italian red made from the Sangiovese grape.

Chicken and Asparagus in White Wine Sauce

This recipe works equally well with green beans or haricots verts in place of asparagus.

Yield: 4 servings (serving size: 1 chicken breast half, about 5 asparagus spears, and about 2 tablespoons sauce)

4 (6-ounce) skinless, boneless chicken breast halves

¾ teaspoon salt

¼ teaspoon freshly ground black pepper

2 tablespoons butter

2.25 ounces all-purpose flour (about ½ cup)

½ cup dry white wine

½ cup fat-free, less-sodium chicken broth

2 garlic cloves, minced

1 pound asparagus spears, trimmed

2 tablespoons chopped fresh parsley

1 tablespoon fresh lemon juice

1. Place each chicken breast half between 2 sheets of heavy-duty plastic wrap; pound to ¼-inch thickness using a meat mallet or small heavy skillet. Sprinkle chicken breasts evenly with salt and freshly ground black pepper.
2. Melt butter in a large nonstick skillet over medium-high heat. Place flour in a shallow dish. Dredge chicken in flour. Add chicken to pan; cook 3 minutes on each side or until done. Remove chicken from pan; keep warm. Add wine, broth, and garlic to pan, scraping pan to loosen browned bits; cook 2 minutes. Add asparagus; cover and cook 3 minutes or until asparagus is crisp-tender. Remove from heat; stir in parsley and juice. Serve asparagus and sauce with chicken.

CALORIES 289; FAT 8g (sat 4.2g, mono 2g, poly 0.8g); PROTEIN 43g; CARB 10.5g; FIBER 2.8g; CHOL 114mg; IRON 4.3mg; SODIUM 648mg; CALC 59mg

QUICK TIP

To speed up the process in step one, purchase thinly sliced chicken breasts (sometimes labeled chicken breast cutlets or chicken breast fillets).

Prosciutto and Fontina–Stuffed Chicken Breasts

Serve a crisp green salad with apple wedges to contrast the creamy, melted cheese filling inside the chicken.

Yield: 4 servings (serving size: 1 stuffed chicken breast half)

Cooking spray

1 ounce chopped prosciutto

1½ teaspoons minced fresh rosemary

2 garlic cloves, minced

¼ cup (1 ounce) shredded fontina cheese

4 (6-ounce) skinless, boneless chicken breast halves

¼ teaspoon freshly ground black pepper

42 saltine crackers (about 1 sleeve)

2.25 ounces all-purpose flour (about ½ cup)

2 large egg whites

1 tablespoon Dijon mustard

2 tablespoons canola oil

1. Heat a large nonstick skillet over medium-high heat. Coat pan with cooking spray. Add prosciutto to pan; sauté 2 minutes or until browned. Add rosemary and garlic to pan; sauté 1 minute. Spoon prosciutto mixture into a bowl; cool to room temperature. Stir in fontina cheese; set aside.

2. Cut a horizontal slit through thickest portion of each chicken breast half to form a pocket. Stuff about 2 tablespoons prosciutto mixture into each pocket; press lightly to flatten. Sprinkle chicken evenly with pepper.

3. Place crackers in a food processor; process 2 minutes or until finely ground. Place cracker crumbs in a shallow dish. Place flour in another shallow dish. Combine egg whites and mustard in another shallow dish, stirring mixture with a whisk.

4. Working with one chicken breast half at a time, dredge chicken in flour, shaking off excess. Dip chicken into egg white mixture, allowing excess to drip off. Coat chicken completely with cracker crumbs. Set aside. Repeat procedure with remaining chicken, flour, egg white mixture, and cracker crumbs.

5. Heat pan over medium-high heat. Add oil to pan, swirling to coat. Add chicken to pan; reduce heat to medium, and cook 10 minutes on each side or until browned and done.

CALORIES 381; FAT 14g (sat 3g, mono 6.4g, poly 2.9g); PROTEIN 46.6g; CARB 14.1g; FIBER 0.6g; CHOL 113mg; IRON 2.4mg; SODIUM 591mg; CALC 74mg

QUICK TIP

Finely ground saltine cracker crumbs create a golden crust. You can save the step of making your own crumbs if your supermarket stocks cracker meal; if so, start with about 1½ cups.

Citrus Chicken

This spicy sauce works equally well with fish or pork.

Yield: 4 servings

¼ cup orange juice

½ teaspoon grated lime rind

2 tablespoons fresh lime juice

2 tablespoons chopped fresh thyme

2 teaspoons bottled minced garlic

1 teaspoon grated orange rind

¼ teaspoon salt

⅛ teaspoon ground red pepper

1 pound skinless, boneless chicken breast cutlets

1 tablespoon olive oil

Cooking spray

6 cups bagged prewashed baby spinach

1. Combine first 8 ingredients in a small bowl, stirring well with a whisk. Pour ¼ cup juice mixture into a large zip-top plastic bag. Add chicken to bag. Seal; let stand 5 minutes. Add oil to remaining juice mixture; stir well with a whisk.
2. Heat a large nonstick skillet over medium-high heat. Coat pan with cooking spray. Remove chicken from bag; discard marinade. Add chicken to pan; cook 4 minutes on each side or until done. Place 1½ cups spinach on each of 4 plates. Divide chicken evenly among servings; top each serving with 1 tablespoon juice mixture.

CALORIES 183; FAT 4.9g (sat 0.9g, mono 2.8g, poly 0.7g); PROTEIN 27.4g; CARB 7.1g; FIBER 2.1g; CHOL 66mg; IRON 2.3mg; SODIUM 278mg; CALC 50mg

INGREDIENT TIP

Be sure to wash the limes before grating or squeezing. When grating, remove only the colored part of the peel; the white part is bitter. You'll get more juice out of a lime if you bring it to room temperature before squeezing the juice.

Peanut-Crusted Chicken with Pineapple Salsa

Serve with steamed broccoli and warm rolls to complete the dinner.

Yield: 4 servings (serving size: 1 cutlet and ¼ cup salsa)

1 cup chopped fresh pineapple

2 tablespoons chopped fresh cilantro

1 tablespoon finely chopped red onion

⅓ cup unsalted, dry-roasted peanuts

1 (1-ounce) slice white bread

½ teaspoon salt

⅛ teaspoon black pepper

4 (4-ounce) chicken breast cutlets

1½ teaspoons canola oil

Cooking spray

Cilantro sprigs (optional)

1. Combine first 3 ingredients in a small bowl, tossing well.

2. Place peanuts and bread slice in a food processor; process until finely chopped. Sprinkle salt and pepper evenly over chicken. Dredge chicken in breadcrumb mixture.

3. Heat oil in a large nonstick skillet over medium-high heat. Coat pan with cooking spray. Add chicken to pan; cook 2 minutes on each side or until done. Serve chicken with pineapple mixture. Garnish with cilantro sprigs, if desired.

CALORIES 219; FAT 7.4g (sat 1.1g, mono 3.4g, poly 2.1g); PROTEIN 28.9g; CARB 9.1g; FIBER 1.3g; CHOL 66mg; IRON 1.2mg; SODIUM 398mg; CALC 27mg

QUICK TIP

Pick up a container of fresh pineapple chunks in the produce section of the supermarket; chop into ½-inch pieces for the salsa.

Pan-Fried Chicken

The key to success with this recipe is even heat. If the oil gets too hot, the chicken may brown too quickly before fully cooking. You can lower the heat, or brown the chicken on the stovetop and then cook in a 350° oven until done. If the oil is not hot enough, the chicken will absorb too much of it. Omit spices in the breading, if you prefer.

Yield: 4 servings (serving size: 1 chicken breast half or 1 thigh and 1 drumstick)

4.5 ounces all-purpose flour
(about 1 cup)

2.25 ounces whole wheat flour
(about ½ cup)

1 teaspoon ground ginger

½ teaspoon hot paprika

½ teaspoon ground cinnamon

½ teaspoon freshly ground nutmeg

½ teaspoon fine sea salt

2 bone-in chicken breast halves,
skinned

2 bone-in chicken thighs, skinned

2 chicken drumsticks, skinned

¼ cup peanut oil

1. Sift together first 6 ingredients; place mixture in a large zip-top plastic bag. Sprinkle salt evenly over chicken. Add chicken, one piece at a time, to bag; seal. Shake bag to coat chicken. Remove chicken from bag, shaking off excess flour. Place chicken on a cooling rack; place rack in a jelly-roll pan. Reserve remaining flour mixture. Loosely cover chicken; chill 1½ hours. Let chicken stand at room temperature 30 minutes. Return chicken, one piece at a time, to flour mixture, shaking bag to coat chicken. Discard excess flour mixture.

2. Heat peanut oil in a large skillet over medium-high heat. Add chicken to pan. Reduce heat to medium-low, and cook 25 minutes or until done, carefully turning every 5 minutes.

3. Line a clean cooling rack with brown paper bags; arrange chicken in a single layer on bags. Let stand 5 minutes.

CALORIES 245; FAT 10.1g (sat 2g, mono 4.1g, poly 3g); PROTEIN 28.2g; CARB 9g; FIBER 0.8g; CHOL 87mg; IRON 1.8mg; SODIUM 240mg; CALC 17mg

Honey-Molasses Chicken Drumsticks

The zesty chicken and sauce are good warm right out of the pan but will keep for up to two days in the refrigerator.

Yield: 6 servings (serving size: 1 drumstick)

1 tablespoon brown sugar

2 tablespoons water

2 tablespoons honey

2 tablespoons balsamic vinegar

1 tablespoon Dijon mustard

1 tablespoon molasses

1 teaspoon minced garlic

1 teaspoon olive oil

6 chicken drumsticks, skinned

½ teaspoon kosher salt

¼ teaspoon freshly ground black pepper

1. Combine first 7 ingredients, stirring with a whisk.

2. Heat oil in a large nonstick skillet over medium-high heat. Sprinkle chicken with salt and pepper. Add chicken to pan, browning on all sides. Add honey mixture to pan, turning chicken to coat. Reduce heat to medium-low. Cover and cook 15 minutes or until chicken is done, turning chicken every 5 minutes. Uncover and cook an additional 1 minute or until honey mixture is thick and a mahogany color, and chicken is well coated. Remove from heat; cool 15 minutes. Cover and chill.

CALORIES 180; FAT 7.2g (sat 1.8g, mono 3g, poly 1.6g); PROTEIN 16.7g; CARB 11.9g; FIBER 0.1g; CHOL 53mg; IRON 1.3mg; SODIUM 291mg; CALC 24mg

INGREDIENT TIP

Molasses is a by-product of the sugar-refining process. Boiling the juices extracted from

sugarcane and sugar beets transforms them into a syrup from which sugar crystals are extracted. The liquid left behind is molasses.

Jamaican Chicken Thighs

Reasonably priced chicken thighs make a Caribbean-accented meal when seasoned with classic island spices and sautéed. Serve alongside peaches tossed with lime juice or fresh pineapple with cilantro.

Yield: 4 servings (serving size: 2 thighs)

2 teaspoons garlic powder

1 teaspoon onion powder

½ teaspoon ground ginger

½ teaspoon dried thyme

½ teaspoon ground allspice

¼ teaspoon salt

¼ teaspoon ground nutmeg

¼ teaspoon ground red pepper

⅛ teaspoon freshly ground black pepper

8 skinless, boneless chicken thighs

Cooking spray

1. Combine first 9 ingredients in a small bowl. Rub spice mixture evenly over chicken. Heat a large nonstick skillet over medium-high heat. Coat pan with cooking spray. Add chicken, and cook 5 minutes on each side or until done.

CALORIES 175; FAT 5.5g (sat 1.4g, mono 1.7g, poly 1.4g); PROTEIN 27.5g; CARB 2.2g; FIBER 0.6g; CHOL 115mg; IRON 1.7mg; SODIUM 265mg; CALC 22mg

Chicken with 40 Cloves of Garlic

Roasting softens the flavor of garlic and makes it easy to spread over the baguette slices. Serve with steamed asparagus.

Yield: 8 servings (serving size: about 4 ounces chicken, 2 tablespoons sauce, 5 garlic cloves, and 3 bread slices)

2 (3-pound) whole chickens

1 tablespoon butter

1 tablespoon extra-virgin olive oil

½ teaspoon salt

¼ teaspoon freshly ground black pepper

40 garlic cloves, peeled

1¼ cups fat-free, less-sodium chicken broth

1 cup dry white wine

24 (¼-inch-thick) slices diagonally cut French bread baguette

Chopped fresh flat-leaf parsley (optional)

1. Remove and discard giblets and neck from chickens. Rinse chickens with cold water; pat dry. Trim excess fat; remove skin. Cut each chicken into 8 pieces. Combine butter and oil in a 12-inch nonstick skillet over medium-high heat. Sprinkle salt and pepper evenly over chicken pieces. Add half of chicken pieces to pan; cook 2 minutes on each side or until golden. Remove chicken from pan; keep warm. Repeat procedure with remaining chicken.

2. Reduce heat to medium. Add garlic; cook 1 minute or until garlic begins to brown, stirring frequently. Arrange chicken on top of garlic. Add broth and wine; cover and cook 25 minutes or until chicken is done.

3. Remove chicken from pan; keep warm. Increase heat to medium-high; cook 10 minutes or until liquid is reduced to about 1 cup. Serve sauce and garlic with chicken and bread. Garnish with chopped parsley, if desired.

CALORIES 343; FAT 13.7g (sat 3.6g, mono 4.9g, poly 3.4g); PROTEIN 29.6g; CARB 24.2g; FIBER 2g; CHOL 111mg; IRON 2.3mg; SODIUM 468mg; CALC 58mg

INGREDIENT TIP

One of the basic tenets of French cuisine is making full use of ingredients—hence, whole chickens in this recipe. In a pinch, you can substitute 6 pounds of chicken pieces.

roasted, oven-baked & fried

Chicken-Chile Tostadas

If you can't find ground chicken, grind your own by putting raw skinless, boneless chicken in a food processor. Pulse with the chopping blade until roughly chopped for the best texture. Tortillas are usually fried for tostadas, but here they're baked for extra crunch.

Yield: 4 servings

1 tablespoon olive oil

1 cup prechopped onion

1 teaspoon bottled minced garlic

½ teaspoon ground cumin

½ teaspoon ground chipotle chile pepper

¼ teaspoon ground cinnamon

1 pound ground chicken breast

½ cup bottled fat-free salsa

¼ cup water

½ teaspoon salt

2 tablespoons chopped fresh cilantro

1 teaspoon lime juice

4 (6-inch) corn tortillas

1 cup shredded iceberg lettuce

1 cup (4 ounces) preshredded reduced-fat Mexican cheese blend or cheddar cheese

¼ cup reduced-fat sour cream

1. Preheat oven to 400°.

2. Heat oil in a large nonstick skillet over medium-high heat. Add onion and garlic; sauté 2 minutes or until onion begins to soften. Add cumin, chipotle, and cinnamon; cook 30 seconds, stirring constantly. Add chicken; cook 4 minutes or until chicken is no longer pink, stirring to crumble. Add salsa, water, and salt; cook 3 minutes or until slightly thickened. Stir in cilantro and lime juice; remove from heat.

3. While chicken cooks, place tortillas directly on oven rack; bake at 400° for 5 minutes or until slightly crisp. Place 1 tortilla on each of 4 plates; top each tortilla with ¼ cup lettuce, ¾ cup chicken mixture, ¼ cup cheese, and 1 tablespoon sour cream.

CALORIES 341; FAT 11.6g (sat 5.2g, mono 3g, poly 0.9g); PROTEIN 35.9g; CARB 21.7g; FIBER 2.6g; CHOL 86mg; IRON 1.6mg; SODIUM 751mg; CALC 296mg

Chicken and Basil Calzones

Ground chicken breast is a lean alternative to beef. Substitute ground sirloin, if you prefer. Serve with a spinach and orange salad to round out your meal.

Yield: 4 servings (serving size: 1 calzone)

Cooking spray

2 garlic cloves, minced

1 pound ground chicken breast

¾ cup prepared pizza sauce

¼ teaspoon crushed red pepper

¼ cup chopped fresh basil

1 (13.8-ounce) can refrigerated pizza crust dough

½ cup (2 ounces) shredded part-skim mozzarella cheese

1. Preheat oven to 425°.

2. Heat a large nonstick skillet over medium-high heat. Coat pan with cooking spray. Add garlic and chicken to pan; sauté 5 minutes or until chicken is no longer pink, stirring to crumble. Stir in pizza sauce and pepper. Reduce heat, and simmer 5 minutes, stirring occasionally. Remove from heat; stir in basil. Let stand 10 minutes.

3. Unroll dough onto a baking sheet coated with cooking spray; cut dough into quarters. Pat each portion into an 8 x 6–inch rectangle. Divide chicken mixture evenly among rectangles; top each serving with 2 tablespoons cheese. Working with one rectangle at a time, fold dough in half over filling, pinching edges to seal. Repeat procedure with remaining rectangles. Bake at 425° for 12 minutes or until golden.

CALORIES 459; FAT 7.1g (sat 1.8g, mono 1g, poly 0.4g); PROTEIN 39.1g; CARB 56.4g; FIBER 3g; CHOL 74mg; IRON 3.7mg; SODIUM 919mg; CALC 111mg

QUICK TIP

If you're pressed for time, use canned Mandarin oranges packed in light syrup in place of fresh orange sections in your salad. Be sure to drain them first.

Three-Cheese Chicken Penne Florentine

Fresh spinach, chicken, and a combination of cheeses make this dish comforting enough for the last days of winter yet fresh enough for the first days of spring.

Yield: 8 servings (serving size: about 1 cup)

1 teaspoon olive oil

Cooking spray

3 cups thinly sliced mushrooms

1 cup chopped onion

1 cup chopped red bell pepper

3 cups chopped fresh spinach

1 tablespoon chopped fresh oregano

¼ teaspoon freshly ground black pepper

1 (16-ounce) carton 2% low-fat cottage cheese

4 cups hot cooked penne (about 8 ounces uncooked tube-shaped pasta)

2 cups shredded roasted skinless, boneless chicken breast

1 cup (4 ounces) shredded reduced-fat sharp cheddar cheese, divided

½ cup (2 ounces) grated fresh Parmesan cheese, divided

½ cup 2% reduced-fat milk

1 (10¾-ounce) can condensed reduced-fat, reduced-sodium cream of chicken soup, undiluted

1. Preheat oven to 425°.

2. Heat olive oil in a large nonstick skillet coated with cooking spray over medium-high heat. Add mushrooms, onion, and bell pepper; sauté 4 minutes or until tender. Add spinach, oregano, and black pepper; sauté 3 minutes or just until spinach wilts.

3. Place cottage cheese in a food processor; process until very smooth. Combine spinach mixture, cottage cheese, pasta, chicken, ¾ cup cheddar cheese, ¼ cup Parmesan cheese, milk, and soup in a large bowl. Spoon mixture into a 2-quart baking dish coated with cooking spray. Sprinkle with remaining ¼ cup cheddar cheese and remaining ¼ cup Parmesan cheese. Bake at 425° for 25 minutes or until lightly browned and bubbly.

CALORIES 345; FAT 9.7g (sat 5.1g, mono 3.1g, poly 1g); PROTEIN 31.7g; CARB 32.9g; FIBER 2.1g; CHOL 56mg; IRON 2mg; SODIUM 532mg; CALC 275mg

QUICK TIP

You can also cook the pasta mixture in individual 8-ounce ramekins; bake for 15 minutes.

Roast Chicken Chimichangas

This Mexican-inspired dish is a great way to use leftover chicken. The chimichangas are oven-browned instead of deep-fried, making them a healthful weeknight choice compared to traditional restaurant offerings.

Yield: 6 servings (serving size: 1 chimichanga and about 4 teaspoons salsa)

2½ cups shredded roasted skinless, boneless chicken breast

1 cup (4 ounces) crumbled queso fresco cheese

¼ cup chopped green onions

1 teaspoon dried oregano

¼ teaspoon ground cumin

1 garlic clove, minced

1 (4.5-ounce) can chopped green chiles, drained

1 (16-ounce) can fat-free refried beans

6 (8-inch) flour tortillas

Cooking spray

½ cup bottled green salsa

1. Preheat oven to 500°.

2. Combine first 7 ingredients in a large bowl; toss well.

3. Spread ¼ cup beans down center of each tortilla. Top each tortilla with ⅔ cup chicken mixture; roll up. Place rolls, seam sides down, on a large baking sheet coated with cooking spray. Coat tops of chimichangas with cooking spray. Bake at 500° for 7 minutes. Serve with salsa.

CALORIES 380; FAT 9.7g (sat 3.1g, mono 4.1g, poly 1.6g); PROTEIN 28.8g; CARB 42.5g; FIBER 6.5g; CHOL 55mg; IRON 3.8mg; SODIUM 728mg; CALC 157mg

INGREDIENT TIP

The chimichanga filling uses queso fresco. If it's not available, try shredded Monterey Jack.

Chicken Enchiladas with Salsa Verde

A squeeze of lime juice brightens the flavor of this hearty Mexican dish. The enchiladas are mild, so serve with hot sauce, if desired. If you can't find queso fresco, use ¼ cup shredded Monterey Jack cheese or Monterey Jack with jalapeño peppers.

Yield: 4 servings (serving size: 2 enchiladas and 1 lime wedge)

1 cup chopped onion

¼ cup chopped fresh cilantro

2 garlic cloves, minced

1 (7-ounce) bottle salsa verde (such as Herdez)

2 cups shredded cooked chicken breast

⅓ cup (3 ounces) ⅓-less-fat cream cheese, softened

1 cup fat-free, less-sodium chicken broth

8 (6-inch) corn tortillas

Cooking spray

¼ cup (1 ounce) crumbled queso fresco

½ teaspoon chili powder

4 lime wedges

Cilantro sprigs (optional)

1. Preheat oven to 425°.

2. Place first 4 ingredients in a blender; process until smooth. Combine chicken and cream cheese in a large bowl. Stir in ½ cup salsa mixture. Reserve remaining salsa mixture.

3. Bring broth to a simmer in a medium skillet. Working with one tortilla at a time, add tortilla to pan; cook 20 seconds or until moist, turning once. Remove tortilla; drain on paper towels. Spoon about ¼ cup chicken mixture down center of tortilla; roll up. Place tortilla, seam side down, in an 11 x 7–inch baking dish coated with cooking spray. Repeat procedure with remaining tortillas, broth, and chicken mixture.

4. Pour remaining salsa mixture over enchiladas; sprinkle evenly with queso fresco and chili powder. Bake at 425° for 18 minutes or until thoroughly heated. Serve with lime wedges. Garnish with cilantro sprigs, if desired.

CALORIES 327; FAT 9.5g (sat 4.4g, mono 2.9g, poly 1.3g); PROTEIN 28.5g; CARB 31g; FIBER 3.3g; CHOL 78mg; IRON 1.8mg; SODIUM 493mg; CALC 149mg

QUICK TIP

Buy a rotisserie chicken at the supermarket, and use the breast meat for this recipe. Use any leftover meat for sandwiches.

Aunt Liz's Chicken Spaghetti Casserole

Bake a frozen casserole, covered, for 55 minutes at 350°; uncover and bake an additional 10 minutes or until hot and bubbly.

Yield: 2 casseroles, 4 servings each (serving size: about 1 cup)

2 cups chopped cooked chicken breast

2 cups uncooked spaghetti noodles, broken into 2-inch pieces (about 7 ounces)

1 cup (¼-inch-thick) slices celery

1 cup chopped red bell pepper

1 cup chopped onion

1 cup fat-free, less-sodium chicken broth

½ teaspoon salt

¼ teaspoon freshly ground black pepper

2 (10.75-ounce) cans condensed 30% reduced-sodium 98% fat-free cream of mushroom soup, undiluted

Cooking spray

1 cup (4 ounces) shredded cheddar cheese, divided

1. Preheat oven to 350°.

2. Combine first 5 ingredients in a large bowl. Combine broth, salt, pepper, and soup in a medium bowl, stirring with a whisk. Add soup mixture to chicken mixture; toss. Divide mixture evenly between 2 (8-inch) square or (2-quart) baking dishes coated with cooking spray. Sprinkle ½ cup cheese over each casserole. Cover with foil coated with cooking spray. Bake at 350° for 35 minutes. Uncover and bake an additional 10 minutes.

CALORIES 261; FAT 7.8g (sat 3.9g, mono 2.2g, poly 1.1g); PROTEIN 19g; CARB 28g; FIBER 2.1g; CHOL 47mg; IRON 1.8mg; SODIUM 652mg; CALC 134mg

Biscuit-Topped Chicken Potpie

Serve a homemade potpie that tastes just like Mom's, but cooks in a fraction of the time.

Yield: 6 servings (serving size: 1½ cups)

1 tablespoon butter

2 cups chopped leek

¼ cup chopped shallot

¾ teaspoon chopped fresh or
¼ teaspoon dried thyme

1½ cups refrigerated diced potatoes
with onions (such as Simply
Potatoes)

⅓ cup dry white wine

1 teaspoon Dijon mustard

1 (14-ounce) can fat-free,
less-sodium chicken broth

2 cups chopped roasted chicken
breast

1½ cups frozen mixed vegetables

¼ teaspoon salt

¼ teaspoon freshly ground black
pepper

1½ tablespoons cornstarch

2 tablespoons water

⅔ cup half-and-half

Cooking spray

1¼ cups low-fat baking mix (such
as Bisquick Heart Smart)

½ cup fat-free milk

1 large egg white, lightly beaten

1. Preheat oven to 425°.

2. Melt butter in a large nonstick skillet over medium-high heat. Add leek, shallot, and thyme; sauté 2 minutes. Add potatoes; sauté 2 minutes. Add wine; cook 1 minute or until liquid evaporates. Stir in mustard and broth; bring to a boil. Cook 4 minutes, stirring occasionally. Stir in chicken, mixed vegetables, salt, and pepper; cook 1 minute. Combine cornstarch and 2 tablespoons water in a small bowl, stirring with a whisk. Add cornstarch mixture and half-and-half to pan. Reduce heat, and simmer 2 minutes, stirring constantly. Spoon mixture into a 13 x 9–inch baking dish coated with cooking spray.

3. Lightly spoon baking mix into dry measuring cups; level with a knife. Combine baking mix, milk, and egg in a medium bowl, stirring with a whisk. Spoon batter over chicken mixture; spread evenly to cover. Bake at 425° for 20 minutes or until topping is golden and filling is bubbly. Let stand 10 minutes.

CALORIES 348; FAT 9.2g (sat 4.1g, mono 2.2g, poly 0.9g); PROTEIN 23.5g; CARB 43.3g; FIBER 4.4g; CHOL 55mg; IRON 3.1mg; SODIUM 634mg; CALC 131mg

QUICK TIP

To clean leeks, chop and place in a strainer; rinse under running water.

Chicken Potpie

To make only three servings, use 1½ tablespoons flour, cut the phyllo sheets into quarters, and scale remaining ingredients down by half. Bake the potpies in three (10-ounce) ramekins. (Tuck one quarter of phyllo sheets on top of each ramekin; discard remaining quarter.) Bake 15 minutes or until tops are golden.

Yield: 6 servings

2 tablespoons butter

2 tablespoons olive oil

3 cups diced red potato (about 1 pound)

2 cups diced onion

2 cups sliced mushrooms (about 8 ounces)

1 cup diced celery

1 cup diced carrot

¼ cup chopped fresh parsley

2 teaspoons chopped fresh thyme

6½ tablespoons all-purpose flour

3 cups fat-free milk

½ cup fat-free, less-sodium chicken broth

2 cups chopped cooked chicken breast (about 12 ounces)

1 cup frozen green peas

1 teaspoon salt

½ teaspoon freshly ground black pepper

6 (14 x 9-inch) sheets frozen phyllo dough, thawed

Cooking spray

1. Preheat oven to 375°.

2. Melt butter in a large saucepan over medium-high heat; add oil. Add potatoes and next 6 ingredients, and sauté 5 minutes. Reduce heat to low; sprinkle flour over vegetables. Cook 5 minutes, stirring frequently. Stir in milk and broth. Increase heat to medium-high; bring to a boil. Reduce heat, and simmer 5 minutes or until thickened. Add chicken, peas, salt, and pepper.

3. Spoon mixture into a 3-quart baking dish. Place 1 phyllo sheet on a large cutting board or work surface (cover remaining dough to keep from drying); lightly spray with cooking spray. Repeat layers with cooking spray and remaining phyllo. Place phyllo layers loosely on top of mixture in dish. Place dish on a baking sheet. Bake at 375° for 30 minutes or until top is golden.

CALORIES 354; FAT 11.2g (sat 3.8g, mono 5.3g, poly 1.2g); PROTEIN 24.2g; CARB 40g; FIBER 4.4g; CHOL 52mg; IRON 2.5mg; SODIUM 680mg; CALC 209mg

QUICK TIP

To reduce prep time, look for prechopped vegetables in the supermarket.

Cheesy Chicken Enchiladas

Serve with a salad of fresh mango, jicama, and shredded lettuce topped with a lime vinaigrette.

Yield: 8 servings (serving size: 1 enchilada)

2½ cups chopped cooked chicken breast

2 cups (8 ounces) preshredded reduced-fat 4-cheese Mexican blend cheese

1⅔ cups plain low-fat yogurt

⅓ cup butter, melted

¼ cup chopped onion

1 teaspoon minced garlic

¼ teaspoon freshly ground black pepper

1 (10¾-ounce) can condensed reduced-fat, reduced-sodium cream of chicken soup (such as Healthy Request), undiluted

1 (4.5-ounce) can chopped green chiles, drained

8 (8-inch) flour tortillas

1 tablespoon canola oil

Cooking spray

½ cup (2 ounces) finely shredded reduced-fat sharp cheddar cheese

¼ cup chopped green onions

1. Preheat oven to 350°.

2. Combine first 9 ingredients in a large bowl. Remove 1 cup chicken mixture; set mixture aside.

3. Heat a large skillet over medium-high heat. Working with one tortilla at a time, brush oil over both sides of tortilla. Add tortilla to pan; cook 5 seconds on each side or until toasted and soft. Remove from pan; arrange ½ cup chicken mixture down center of tortilla. Roll jelly-roll style; place filled tortilla, seam side down, in a 13 x 9–inch baking dish coated with cooking spray. Repeat procedure with remaining 7 tortillas, remaining oil, and remaining chicken mixture. Spread reserved 1 cup chicken mixture evenly over enchiladas. Cover and bake at 350° for 20 minutes. Uncover; sprinkle evenly with cheddar cheese and green onions; bake an additional 5 minutes or until cheese melts.

CALORIES 454; FAT 20.3g (sat 10.4g, mono 6.7g, poly 1.5g); PROTEIN 30.8g; CARB 36.6g; FIBER 2.2g; CHOL 73mg; IRON 2.3mg; SODIUM 757mg; CALC 347mg

WINE TIP

Just as a crunchy green salad with mango will complement Cheesy Chicken Enchiladas, so too will a crisp, tropical fruit-filled California chardonnay.

Herbed Stuffed Chicken Breasts

Dish up a company-worthy entrée that calls for only four ingredients, plus salt and pepper. Choose roasted asparagus as a bright, fresh partner for this main dish. Complete the meal with a baguette slice and a glass of crisp white wine.

Yield: 4 servings (serving size: 1 chicken breast half and about 1 tablespoon pan juices)

¼ cup (2 ounces) goat cheese

½ teaspoon chopped fresh rosemary

2 ounces Canadian bacon, finely chopped

4 (6-ounce) skinless, boneless chicken breasts

¼ teaspoon salt

¼ teaspoon freshly ground black pepper

Cooking spray

1. Preheat oven to 400°.

2. Combine first 3 ingredients in a small bowl. Cut a horizontal slit through thickest portion of each chicken breast half to form a pocket. Stuff about 3 tablespoons cheese mixture into each pocket; close opening with a wooden pick. Sprinkle chicken evenly with salt and pepper.

3. Heat a large cast-iron skillet over medium-high heat. Coat pan with cooking spray. Add chicken to pan; cook 4 minutes. Turn chicken over; place pan in oven. Bake at 400° for 25 minutes or until chicken is done. Let stand 5 minutes. Discard wooden picks. Cut chicken diagonally into ½-inch-thick slices. Serve with pan juices.

CALORIES 302; FAT 13.5g (sat 5.1g, mono 4.8g, poly 2.2g); PROTEIN 42.1g; CARB 0.5g; FIBER 0g; CHOL 116mg; IRON 1.7mg; SODIUM 486mg; CALC 40mg

Feta, Herb, and Sun-Dried Tomato–Stuffed Chicken

Sun-dried tomatoes and fresh basil temper tangy feta in a savory chicken breast stuffing. Serve with quick-cooking orzo pasta tossed with fresh parsley.

Yield: 4 servings (serving size: 1 packet)

2 cups water

½ cup sun-dried tomatoes, packed without oil

½ cup (2 ounces) crumbled feta cheese

2 teaspoons chopped fresh basil

1 teaspoon chopped fresh oregano

½ teaspoon minced garlic

¾ teaspoon freshly ground black pepper, divided

4 (6-ounce) skinless, boneless chicken breast halves

½ teaspoon kosher salt

2 tablespoons butter

½ teaspoon grated lemon rind

¼ cup fat-free, less-sodium chicken broth

2 teaspoons thinly sliced fresh basil (optional)

1. Preheat oven to 425°.
2. Bring 2 cups water to a boil in a small saucepan; add tomatoes. Remove from heat; cover and let stand 5 minutes. Drain and slice into thin strips. Combine tomatoes, cheese, 2 teaspoons chopped basil, oregano, garlic, and ¼ teaspoon pepper in a small bowl.
3. Place chicken breast halves between 2 sheets of heavy-duty plastic wrap, and pound each piece to an even thickness using a meat mallet or small heavy skillet. Cut a horizontal slit through one side of each chicken breast half to form a deep pocket. Stuff ¼ cup tomato mixture into each pocket. Sprinkle both sides of chicken with salt and remaining ½ teaspoon pepper.
4. Fold 4 (16 x 12–inch) sheets of heavy-duty aluminum foil in half crosswise. Open foil; place 1½ teaspoons butter on half of each foil sheet. Lay one stuffed chicken breast half on top of each portion of butter. Place ⅛ teaspoon grated lemon rind on top of each stuffed chicken breast half, and drizzle each serving with 1 tablespoon chicken broth. Fold foil over chicken, and tightly seal edges. Place packets on a baking sheet. Bake packets at 425° for 20 minutes. Remove from oven, and let stand 5 minutes. Unfold packets carefully, and thinly slice each chicken breast half. Garnish each serving with ½ teaspoon sliced basil, if desired. Serve immediately.

CALORIES 311; FAT 10.1g (sat 5.7g, mono 2g, poly 0.7g); PROTEIN 43g; CARB 8.2g; FIBER 2.5g; CHOL 121mg; IRON 1.6mg; SODIUM 572mg; CALC 77mg

INGREDIENT TIP

Sun-dried tomatoes add a burst of vivid flavor and nutrition to many dishes. When dried, the naturally sweet taste of Roma, or plum, tomatoes intensifies. Their slightly chewy texture adds richness to the consistency of a dish.

Buttermilk Oven-Fried Chicken with Coleslaw

Cracker meal gives the coating more crunch; look for it on the baking aisle of your supermarket. If you can't find cracker meal, make your own by pulsing 10 saltine crackers in a food processor until they're finely ground. Or place them in a zip-top plastic bag and crush them with a rolling pin. Add a dinner roll to round out the meal.

Yield: 4 servings (serving size: 1 chicken breast half and ¾ cup slaw)

Coleslaw:

4 cups packaged cabbage-and-carrot coleslaw

3 tablespoons fat-free mayonnaise

1½ teaspoons sugar

½ teaspoon celery seeds

1½ teaspoons cider vinegar

⅛ teaspoon salt

Chicken:

1 cup low-fat buttermilk

4 (8-ounce) bone-in chicken breast halves, skinned

1.5 ounces all-purpose flour (about ⅓ cup)

⅓ cup cracker meal

½ teaspoon salt

½ teaspoon freshly ground black pepper

2 tablespoons butter

1. To prepare coleslaw, combine first 6 ingredients; toss to coat. Cover and chill.

2. Preheat oven to 425°.

3. To prepare chicken, combine buttermilk and chicken in a shallow dish, turning to coat.

4. Combine flour and cracker meal in a shallow dish. Transfer chicken from buttermilk to a work surface. Sprinkle chicken evenly with ½ teaspoon salt and pepper. Working with one chicken breast half at a time, dredge chicken in flour mixture, shaking off excess; set aside. Repeat procedure with remaining chicken and flour mixture.

5. Melt butter in a large ovenproof nonstick skillet over medium-high heat. Add chicken to pan, meat side down; cook 4 minutes or until golden brown. Turn chicken over, and bake at 425° for 32 minutes or until a thermometer registers 165°. Serve with coleslaw.

CALORIES 342; FAT 8.8g (sat 4.5g, mono 2.2g, poly 0.8g); PROTEIN 45.1g; CARB 18.5g; FIBER 2.6g; CHOL 123mg; IRON 2.3mg; SODIUM 672mg; CALC 95mg

Oven-Roasted Chicken Breasts with Artichokes and Toasted Breadcrumbs

If you can't find baby artichokes, use six large globe artichokes instead and cook them a bit longer, just until tender.

Yield: 6 servings (serving size: 1 chicken breast half, 6 artichoke halves, ¼ cup sauce, and about 2½ tablespoons breadcrumbs)

5 quarts water, divided

⅓ cup kosher salt

6 bone-in chicken breast halves, skinned

¼ cup fresh lemon juice

18 baby artichokes

2 tablespoons olive oil, divided

¼ teaspoon freshly ground black pepper

1 tablespoon canola oil

1 cup dry white wine

1 (14-ounce) can fat-free, less-sodium chicken broth

1½ ounces French bread baguette

2 tablespoons chopped fresh flat-leaf parsley

1. Combine 3 quarts water and salt in a Dutch oven, stirring until the salt dissolves. Add chicken to salt mixture. Cover and refrigerate 2 hours.

2. Combine remaining 2 quarts water and juice. Cut off stem of each artichoke to within 1 inch of base; peel stem. Remove bottom leaves and tough outer leaves, leaving tender heart and bottom. Cut each artichoke in half lengthwise; place in lemon water.

3. Heat 1 tablespoon olive oil in a large skillet over medium-high heat. Drain artichokes; pat dry. Add artichokes to pan. Cover and cook 10 minutes or until tender. Uncover and cook an additional 5 minutes or until browned, stirring frequently. Keep warm.

4. Preheat oven to 450°.

5. Remove chicken from salt mixture; discard salt mixture. Pat chicken dry; sprinkle evenly with pepper.

6. Heat canola oil in a large ovenproof skillet over medium-high heat. Wrap handle of pan with foil. Add chicken to pan, meat side down; sauté 1 minute. Bake at 450° for 10 minutes. Turn chicken over; bake an additional 12 minutes or until done. Keep warm.

7. Place a zip-top plastic bag inside a 2-cup glass measure. Pour drippings into bag; let stand 10 minutes (fat will rise to the top). Seal bag; carefully snip off 1 bottom corner of bag. Drain drippings back into pan, stopping before fat layer reaches opening; discard fat.

8. Add white wine to drippings in pan; bring to a boil, scraping pan to loosen browned bits. Reduce heat; simmer until reduced to 1 cup (about 5 minutes). Add broth to pan; simmer until reduced to 1½ cups (about 10 minutes).

9. Reduce oven temperature to 350°. Place bread in food processor; pulse 10 times or until coarse crumbs measure 1 cup. Combine remaining 1 tablespoon olive oil and breadcrumbs in a bowl; toss to coat. Arrange crumbs in a single layer on a baking sheet; bake at 350° for 5 minutes or until golden. Add parsley; toss to combine. Serve chicken with artichokes and sauce. Top with breadcrumbs. Serve immediately.

CALORIES 293; FAT 10.5g (sat 1.8g, mono 5.8g, poly 2.2g); PROTEIN 32.5g; CARB 19.3g; FIBER 7.5g; CHOL 73mg; IRON 3.2mg; SODIUM 835mg; CALC 82mg

Oven-Fried Chicken

Instead of deep-frying the chicken, this recipe calls for browning the chicken pieces in a skillet and then baking them in the oven. So how do you get the traditional crispy crust of fried chicken? Cornmeal. This "secret" ingredient makes the crust extra crisp every time.

Yield: 4 servings (serving size: 1 chicken breast half or 1 drumstick and 1 thigh)

1 cup low-fat buttermilk

2 large egg whites, beaten

4.5 ounces all-purpose flour (about 1 cup)

⅓ cup cornmeal

1 teaspoon salt, divided

¾ teaspoon freshly ground black pepper

¼ teaspoon ground red pepper

2 chicken breast halves, skinned (about 1 pound)

2 chicken thighs, skinned (about ½ pound)

2 chicken drumsticks, skinned (about ½ pound)

2 tablespoons canola oil

Cooking spray

1. Preheat oven to 425°.

2. Cover a large baking sheet with parchment paper. Combine buttermilk and egg whites in a shallow dish; stir well with a whisk. Combine flour, cornmeal, ½ teaspoon salt, black pepper, and red pepper in a separate shallow dish; stir well. Sprinkle chicken evenly with remaining ½ teaspoon salt. Dip chicken in buttermilk mixture; dredge in flour mixture.

3. Heat oil in a large nonstick skillet over medium-high heat. Add chicken to pan; cook 4 minutes on each side or until lightly browned. Place chicken on prepared baking sheet; lightly coat chicken with cooking spray. Bake at 425° for 30 minutes or until chicken is done.

CALORIES 450; FAT 13.8g (sat 2.5g, mono 6.1g, poly 3.6g); PROTEIN 43.5g; CARB 35.3g; FIBER 1.7g; CHOL 109mg; IRON 3.2mg; SODIUM 803mg; CALC 88mg

Oven-Fried Coconut Chicken

The marinade infuses dark-meat chicken with a light coconut flavor; flaked coconut in the breading heightens the nutty taste.

Yield: 4 servings (serving size: 1 thigh and 1 drumstick)

1 tablespoon fresh lime juice

1 tablespoon hot pepper sauce

1 (14-ounce) can light coconut milk

4 (4-ounce) chicken thighs, skinned

4 (4-ounce) chicken drumsticks, skinned

¾ cup panko (Japanese breadcrumbs)

½ cup flaked sweetened coconut

½ teaspoon salt

¼ teaspoon freshly ground black pepper

Cooking spray

1. Combine first 3 ingredients in a large zip-top plastic bag. Add chicken to bag; seal. Marinate in refrigerator 1½ hours, turning bag occasionally.
2. Preheat oven to 400°.
3. Combine panko, flaked coconut, salt, and black pepper in a shallow dish. Remove chicken from marinade; discard marinade. Dredge chicken, 1 piece at a time, in panko mixture. Place chicken on a baking sheet lined with parchment paper. Lightly coat chicken with cooking spray. Bake at 400° for 30 minutes or until golden brown. Carefully turn chicken over; bake an additional 30 minutes or until done.

CALORIES 256; FAT 8.6g (sat 4.4g, mono 1.6g, poly 1.2g); PROTEIN 27.7g; CARB 15.6g; FIBER 0.8g; CHOL 103mg; IRON 1.6mg; SODIUM 464mg; CALC 18mg

INGREDIENT TIP

Panko (Japanese bread-crumbs) gives this oven-fried chicken a crispy exterior. If you're looking for panko, try your supermarket's ethnic food aisle.

Vanilla Balsamic Chicken

After scraping the seeds for the sauce, add the vanilla bean pod to a canister of sugar. The scent of the bean will permeate the sugar. Serve the chicken with a tossed green salad.

Yield: 8 servings (serving size: 2 thighs)

½ cup fat-free, less-sodium chicken broth

½ cup balsamic vinegar

¼ cup finely chopped shallots

¼ cup packed brown sugar

¼ teaspoon grated orange rind

¼ cup fresh orange juice

1 (2-inch) piece vanilla bean, split lengthwise

¾ teaspoon salt, divided

16 skinless, boneless chicken thighs (about 2 pounds)

Cooking spray

½ teaspoon freshly ground black pepper

Orange rind strips (optional)

1. Preheat oven to 450°.

2. Combine first 6 ingredients in a small saucepan. Scrape seeds from vanilla bean; stir seeds into broth mixture, reserving the bean for another use. Bring to a boil. Reduce heat, and simmer until reduced to ½ cup (about 20 minutes). Stir in ¼ teaspoon salt.

3. Arrange chicken in a single layer in the bottom of a roasting pan coated with cooking spray. Sprinkle chicken evenly with remaining ½ teaspoon salt and pepper. Bake at 450° for 10 minutes.

4. Brush half of broth mixture over chicken; bake 5 minutes. Brush remaining broth mixture over chicken; bake 15 minutes or until a thermometer registers 180°. Garnish with orange rind, if desired.

CALORIES 209; FAT 5.5g (sat 1.4g, mono 1.7g, poly 1.4g); PROTEIN 27.5g; CARB 10.9g; FIBER 0.2g; CHOL 115mg; IRON 1.8mg; SODIUM 371mg; CALC 29mg

Spicy Honey-Brushed Chicken Thighs

Skinless, boneless thighs cook quickly and are more flavorful than white meat, so they need fewer ingredients. Serve with garlic-roasted potato wedges and a salad or broccolini.

Yield: 4 servings (serving size: 2 thighs)

2 teaspoons garlic powder

2 teaspoons chili powder

1 teaspoon salt

1 teaspoon ground cumin

1 teaspoon paprika

½ teaspoon ground red pepper

8 skinless, boneless chicken thighs

Cooking spray

6 tablespoons honey

2 teaspoons cider vinegar

1. Preheat broiler.

2. Combine first 6 ingredients in a large bowl. Add chicken to bowl; toss to coat. Place chicken on a broiler pan coated with cooking spray. Broil chicken 5 minutes on each side.

3. Combine honey and vinegar in a small bowl, stirring well. Remove chicken from oven; brush ¼ cup honey mixture on chicken. Broil 1 minute. Remove chicken from oven and turn over. Brush chicken with remaining honey mixture. Broil 1 additional minute or until chicken is done.

CALORIES 321; FAT 11g (sat 3g, mono 4.1g, poly 2.5g); PROTEIN 28g; CARB 27.9g; FIBER 0.6g; CHOL 99mg; IRON 2.1mg; SODIUM 676mg; CALC 21mg

Honey-Pomegranate Roasted Chicken Thighs

You can find pomegranate molasses in Middle Eastern and specialty stores. Serve these succulent thighs warm or at room temperature. Garnish with chives, if desired.

Yield: 8 servings (serving size: 2 thighs)

¾ cup honey

⅓ cup finely chopped shallots

¼ cup fresh lemon juice (about 3 small lemons)

1 tablespoon grated lemon rind

2 tablespoons pomegranate molasses

1 teaspoon Worcestershire sauce

1 teaspoon hot sauce

6 garlic cloves, minced

16 chicken thighs (about 4 pounds), skinned

1 tablespoon cornstarch

1 tablespoon water

Cooking spray

1 teaspoon salt

¼ teaspoon freshly ground black pepper

1. Combine first 9 ingredients in a large bowl; marinate in refrigerator 2 hours, stirring occasionally.

2. Preheat oven to 425°.

3. Remove chicken from bowl, reserving marinade. Combine cornstarch and water in a small bowl. Place reserved marinade in a small saucepan; bring to a boil. Stir in cornstarch mixture, and cook 3 minutes or until thickened, stirring frequently. Remove from heat. Place chicken on a broiler pan coated with cooking spray; sprinkle with salt and pepper. Bake at 425° for 30 minutes or until chicken is done, basting with reserved marinade every 10 minutes.

CALORIES 378; FAT 13.1g (sat 3.7g, mono 5g, poly 3g); PROTEIN 31.7g; CARB 33.8g; FIBER 0.3g; CHOL 114mg; IRON 2.6mg; SODIUM 416mg; CALC 36mg

Spiced Roasted Chicken

While it's easy enough to buy a rotisserie chicken, roasting chicken at home allows you to control the sodium, flavorings, and quality of ingredients. Preparation is simple, while cooking is hands-off. Serve with a quick carrot-raisin salad and mashed potatoes.

Yield: 4 servings (serving size: about 5 ounces chicken)

1 (3¾-pound) whole roasting chicken

1 teaspoon dried oregano

1 teaspoon cumin seed, crushed

1 teaspoon bottled minced garlic

2 teaspoons olive oil

½ teaspoon salt

½ teaspoon ground cumin

Cooking spray

1. Preheat oven to 375°.

2. Remove and discard giblets and neck from chicken; trim excess fat. Starting at neck cavity, loosen skin from breasts and drumsticks by inserting fingers, gently pushing between skin and meat.

3. Combine oregano, cumin seed, garlic, oil, salt, and ground cumin in a small bowl. Rub seasoning mixture under loosened skin and over breasts and drumsticks. Tie ends of legs together with twine. Lift wing tips up and over back; tuck under chicken. Place chicken, breast side up, on a rack coated with cooking spray, and place rack in a roasting pan.

4. Bake at 375° for 40 minutes.

5. Increase oven temperature to 450° (do not remove chicken from oven); bake an additional 12 minutes or until a thermometer inserted in the meaty part of thigh registers 165°. Remove chicken from pan; let stand 15 minutes. Remove skin from chicken; discard.

CALORIES 185; FAT 6.4g (sat 1.3g, mono 2.9g, poly 1.2g); PROTEIN 29g; CARB 0.8g; FIBER 0.3g; CHOL 92mg; IRON 2.1mg; SODIUM 403mg; CALC 27mg

Lemon-Rosemary Roast Chicken with Potatoes

A green salad is all you'll need to round out the meal. Garnish with rosemary sprigs.

Yield: 4 servings (serving size: 5 ounces chicken, about 1½ cups potatoes, and 1 lemon wedge)

1 (3¾-pound) whole roasting chicken

2 tablespoons olive oil, divided

2 teaspoons chopped fresh rosemary

1 teaspoon grated lemon rind

¾ teaspoon salt, divided

½ teaspoon freshly ground black pepper, divided

3 garlic cloves, minced

Cooking spray

3 baking potatoes, peeled and cut into 1½-inch pieces (about 2 pounds)

4 lemon wedges

1. Preheat oven to 375°.

2. Remove and discard giblets and neck from chicken; trim excess fat. Starting at neck cavity, loosen skin from breasts and drumsticks by inserting fingers, gently pushing between skin and meat.

3. Combine 1 tablespoon oil, rosemary, rind, ½ teaspoon salt, ¼ teaspoon pepper, and garlic in a small bowl. Rub seasoning mixture under loosened skin and over breasts and drumsticks. Tie ends of legs together with twine. Lift wing tips up and over back, and tuck under chicken. Place chicken, breast side up, on a rack coated with cooking spray, and place rack in a roasting pan.

4. Toss potatoes and remaining 1 tablespoon oil. Arrange potato mixture evenly around chicken. Bake at 375° for 40 minutes.

5. Increase oven temperature to 450°, and bake an additional 20 minutes or until a thermometer inserted in meaty part of thigh registers 170°. Remove chicken from pan; let stand 15 minutes. Sprinkle potatoes with remaining ¼ teaspoon salt and ¼ teaspoon pepper.

6. Remove skin from chicken; discard. Carve chicken, and serve with potatoes and lemon wedges.

CALORIES 522; FAT 16.5g (sat 3.5g, mono 8.5g, poly 2.9g); PROTEIN 41.6g; CARB 49.8g; FIBER 5.4g; CHOL 106mg; IRON 4.4mg; SODIUM 568mg; CALC 68mg

WINE TIP

Roast chicken is very versatile with wine, and so are the seasonings used here. In the winter, serve this dish with an earthy red wine like pinot noir. But in the summer, an exuberantly fruity red is best, served slightly chilled.

Herb Roast Chicken

Start with the best-quality chicken you can find. We chose a fresh organic bird. Make your meal complete with smashed potatoes and haricots verts.

Yield: 4 servings (serving size: 1 chicken breast half or 1 thigh and 1 drumstick, and 1 tablespoon drippings)

1 (4½-pound) whole roasting chicken

¾ teaspoon fine sea salt, divided

¾ teaspoon freshly ground black pepper, divided

1 lemon, halved

2 tablespoons butter, softened

2 tablespoons minced shallots

2 teaspoons chopped fresh rosemary

2 teaspoons chopped fresh thyme

Cooking spray

¾ cup water

1. Preheat oven to 450°.

2. Remove giblets and neck from chicken cavity; discard. Trim excess fat from chicken. Loosen skin from breast and drumsticks by inserting fingers, gently pushing between skin and meat. Sprinkle ¼ teaspoon salt and ½ teaspoon pepper inside body cavity. Squeeze lemon juice into body cavity; place lemon halves in body cavity. Combine softened butter, minced shallots, rosemary, and thyme, stirring with a fork until well blended. Combine remaining ½ teaspoon salt and remaining ¼ teaspoon pepper in a small bowl; rub salt mixture evenly under skin over breast and drumstick meat. Rub butter mixture evenly under skin over breast and drumstick meat. Tie ends of legs together with twine. Lift wing tips up and over back, and tuck under chicken.

3. Place chicken, breast side up, on a rack coated with cooking spray; place rack in a roasting pan. Pour ¾ cup water into roasting pan. Bake chicken at 450° for 1 hour or until a thermometer inserted in meaty part of thigh registers 165°. Remove chicken from pan; let stand, breast side down, 15 minutes. Remove skin; discard.

4. Place a large zip-top plastic bag inside a 4-cup glass measure. Pour drippings through a sieve into bag; discard solids. Let drippings stand 10 minutes (fat will rise to the top). Seal bag; carefully snip off 1 bottom corner of bag. Drain drippings into a medium bowl, stopping before fat layer reaches opening; discard fat. Carve chicken; serve with drippings.

CALORIES 222; FAT 11.4g (sat 5.2g, mono 3.5g, poly 1.5g); PROTEIN 26.6g; CARB 2.3g; FIBER 0.2g; CHOL 97mg; IRON 1.3mg; SODIUM 548mg; CALC 23mg

Roasted Chicken with Onions, Potatoes, and Gravy

This recipe first ran in the *Cooking Light* May 2005 issue in a Cooking Class column that profiled Chuck Williams, founder of Williams-Sonoma. It's our hands-down best roast chicken of all time.

Yield: 6 servings (serving size: about 4 ounces chicken, 1⅓ cups onion mixture, and ⅓ cup gravy)

1 (4-pound) whole roasting chicken

1¼ teaspoons salt, divided

¾ teaspoon freshly ground black pepper, divided

4 fresh oregano sprigs

1 lemon, quartered

1 celery stalk, cut into 2-inch pieces

Cooking spray

2 tablespoons butter, melted

2 pounds medium yellow onions, peeled and each cut into 8 wedges

2 pounds small red potatoes, cut into (1-inch) wedges

1 ounce all-purpose flour (about ¼ cup)

1 (14-ounce) can fat-free, less-sodium chicken broth, divided

Lemon wedges (optional)

Oregano sprigs (optional)

1. Preheat oven to 425°.

2. Remove and discard giblets and neck from chicken. Trim excess fat. Starting at neck cavity, loosen skin from breast and drumsticks by inserting fingers, gently pushing between skin and meat. Combine ½ teaspoon salt and ½ teaspoon black pepper; rub under loosened skin and over breast and drumsticks. Place oregano sprigs, quartered lemon, and celery pieces into body cavity. Lift wing tips up and over back; tuck under chicken. Tie legs together with string. Place chicken, breast side up, on the rack of a broiler pan coated with cooking spray.

3. Combine ½ teaspoon salt, remaining ¼ teaspoon pepper, melted butter, onions, and potatoes in a large bowl, and toss well to coat. Arrange onion mixture around chicken on rack. Place rack in pan. Bake at 425° for 20 minutes. Reduce oven temperature to 325° (do not remove pan from oven); bake an additional 1 hour and 10 minutes or until onions and potatoes are tender and a thermometer inserted into meaty part of chicken thigh registers 165°. Set chicken, onions, and potatoes aside; cover and keep warm.

4. Place a zip-top plastic bag inside a 2-cup glass measure. Pour pan drippings into bag; let stand 10 minutes (fat will rise to the top). Seal bag; carefully snip off 1 bottom corner of bag. Drain drippings into a small saucepan, stopping before fat layer reaches opening; discard fat. Combine remaining ¼ teaspoon salt, flour, and ½ cup chicken broth in a small bowl, stirring with a whisk. Add flour mixture and remaining chicken broth to saucepan. Bring to a boil over medium-high heat. Reduce heat to medium; cook 5 minutes or until gravy thickens, stirring frequently with a whisk. Carve chicken; serve with gravy and onion mixture. Garnish with lemon wedges and oregano sprigs, if desired.

CALORIES 430; FAT 11.6g (sat 4.5g, mono 3.8g, poly 2g); PROTEIN 36.9g; CARB 43.7g; FIBER 5.2g; CHOL 113mg; IRON 3.4mg; SODIUM 753mg; CALC 71mg

José's Chicken

Sous-chef Roxana Pareja, of Bayridge Residence in Boston, and her husband, José, created this guest-worthy roast chicken. We think you'll find it worthy of serving to your guests, too.

Yield: 4 servings (serving size: about 4 ounces chicken)

1 (4-pound) whole roasting chicken

1 tablespoon chopped fresh oregano

1 tablespoon chopped fresh parsley

1 tablespoon chopped fresh cilantro

1 teaspoon kosher salt

1 teaspoon ground cumin

2 teaspoons butter, softened

¾ teaspoon freshly ground black pepper

½ teaspoon paprika

2 garlic cloves, crushed

1 small orange, quartered

1 small onion, quartered

Cooking spray

1. Preheat oven to 375°.

2. Remove and discard giblets and neck from chicken; trim excess fat. Starting at neck cavity, loosen skin from breasts and drumsticks by inserting fingers, gently pushing between skin and meat.

3. Combine oregano and next 7 ingredients in a small bowl. Rub oregano mixture under loosened skin and over breasts and drumsticks. Place garlic in body cavity; arrange orange and onion quarters in cavity. Tie ends of legs together with twine. Lift wing tips up and over back; tuck under chicken. Place chicken, breast side up, on a roasting pan coated with cooking spray. Bake at 375° for 1 hour and 20 minutes or until a thermometer inserted into meaty part of thigh registers 165°. Let stand 10 minutes. Discard skin. Remove orange quarters; squeeze juice over chicken. Discard oranges, garlic cloves, and onions.

CALORIES 279; FAT 8.3g (sat 2.8g, mono 2.4g, poly 1.6g); PROTEIN 47.3g; CARB 0.8g; FIBER 0.4g; CHOL 155mg; IRON 2.7mg; SODIUM 659mg; CALC 36mg

salads, sandwiches & pizzas

Chicken, Rice, and Tropical Fruit Salad

You can serve this salad chilled or at room temperature, depending on your preference. You can also substitute lime juice for lemon. Round out your meal with herbed green beans and iced tea.

Yield: 4 servings

1 cup uncooked basmati rice

2 cups cubed skinless, boneless rotisserie chicken breast

1 cup cubed fresh pineapple

1 cup jarred sliced peeled mango, drained and chopped (such as Del Monte SunFresh)

½ cup seedless red grapes, halved

¼ cup sliced almonds, toasted

2 tablespoons finely chopped fresh mint

1½ tablespoons fresh lemon juice

1½ tablespoons canola oil

¼ teaspoon salt

¼ teaspoon freshly ground black pepper

4 romaine lettuce leaves

Mint sprigs (optional)

1. Cook rice according to package directions, omitting salt and fat. Cool. Combine rice and next 5 ingredients.

2. Combine mint, juice, oil, salt, and pepper in a small bowl, stirring with a whisk. Drizzle mint mixture over rice mixture; toss well. Cover and chill. Place 1 lettuce leaf on each of 4 plates. Spoon 1½ cups rice mixture onto each lettuce leaf. Garnish with mint sprigs, if desired.

CALORIES 346; FAT 11.5g (sat 1.4g, mono 6.2g, poly 3g); PROTEIN 25.5g; CARB 36.1g; FIBER 2.8g; CHOL 60mg; IRON 1.6mg; SODIUM 199mg; CALC 45mg

QUICK TIP

Look for peeled, cored, and cubed fresh pineapple and packages of trimmed green beans in the produce section of your supermarket.

Asian Chicken, Noodle, and Vegetable Salad

Mix dark meat with the breast meat, if you like, for added flavor. You'll find Thai sweet chili sauce in Asian and gourmet markets or in your supermarket's ethnic section.

Yield: 4 servings (serving size: 2 cups)

6 ounces uncooked rice noodles

2 cups cubed skinless, boneless rotisserie chicken breast

½ cup matchstick-cut carrots

½ cup chopped green bell pepper

⅓ cup chopped green onions (about 3)

¼ cup canned sliced water chestnuts, drained

¼ cup Thai sweet chili sauce (such as Mae Ploy)

2 tablespoons canola oil

1½ tablespoons rice wine vinegar

1½ tablespoons fresh lemon juice

2 teaspoons low-sodium soy sauce

½ teaspoon grated peeled fresh ginger

2 tablespoons chopped unsalted, dry-roasted peanuts

1. Prepare noodles according to package directions. Drain and cool. Combine noodles, chicken, and next 4 ingredients in a large bowl; toss well.

2. Combine chili sauce and next 5 ingredients in a small bowl, stirring with a whisk. Drizzle chili sauce mixture over noodle mixture; toss gently to coat. Sprinkle with peanuts. Serve immediately.

CALORIES 373; FAT 11.9g (sat 1.5g, mono 6.1g, poly 3.4g); PROTEIN 23.6g; CARB 43.7g; FIBER 1.8g; CHOL 60mg; IRON 2.1mg; SODIUM 368mg; CALC 37mg

QUICK TIP

Spend less time chopping by purchasing matchstick-cut carrots and chopped green bell pepper from the supermarket produce section.

Potato, Chicken, and Fresh Pea Salad

Spring ingredients, such as fingerling potatoes and sugar snap peas, transform rotisserie chicken into a pretty one-dish meal befitting the season. Serve warm, at room temperature, or chilled for maximum versatility. Leftovers make an easy and satisfying lunch.

Yield: 4 servings (serving size: about 1½ cups)

1 pound fingerling potatoes, cut crosswise into 1-inch pieces

2 cups fresh sugar snap peas

2 cups chopped skinless, boneless rotisserie chicken breast

½ cup finely chopped red bell pepper

½ cup finely chopped red onion

2 tablespoons extra-virgin olive oil

2 tablespoons white wine vinegar

1 tablespoon fresh lemon juice

1 tablespoon Dijon mustard

1 teaspoon minced fresh tarragon

1 teaspoon salt

½ teaspoon freshly ground black pepper

1 garlic clove, minced

1. Place potatoes in a large saucepan; cover with cold water. Bring to a boil. Reduce heat, and simmer 10 minutes or until almost tender. Add peas; cook 2 minutes or until peas are crisp-tender. Drain; place vegetables in a large bowl. Add chicken, bell pepper, and onion.

2. Combine oil and remaining ingredients, stirring with a whisk. Drizzle over salad; toss gently to combine.

CALORIES 316; FAT 9.3g (sat 1.7g, mono 5.8g, poly 1.3g); PROTEIN 26.4g; CARB 29.2g; FIBER 3.6g; CHOL 60mg; IRON 2.4mg; SODIUM 680mg; CALC 50mg

INGREDIENT TIP

Sugar snap peas are a springtime favorite. However, look for 6-ounce packages of fresh,

sugar snap peas in the produce section of your supermarket year-round.

Chicken and Feta Tabbouleh

Delicious when eaten right away, the flavors in this meal stand up admirably when it's prepared ahead—making this a good take-to-work lunch, too. Serve with toasted pita wedges or flatbread.

Yield: 4 servings (serving size: 1½ cups)

¾ cup uncooked bulgur

1 cup boiling water

2 cups chopped skinless, boneless rotisserie chicken breast

1 cup chopped plum tomato

1 cup chopped English cucumber

¾ cup chopped fresh parsley

½ cup (2 ounces) crumbled feta cheese

⅓ cup finely chopped green onions

¼ cup chopped fresh mint

2 tablespoons fresh lemon juice

1 tablespoon extra-virgin olive oil

1 teaspoon bottled minced garlic

¼ teaspoon salt

¼ teaspoon ground cumin

¼ teaspoon black pepper

1. Place bulgur in a medium bowl; cover with 1 cup boiling water. Let stand 15 minutes or until liquid is absorbed.

2. Combine chicken and remaining ingredients in a large bowl. Add bulgur to chicken mixture; toss gently to combine.

CALORIES 296; FAT 9.5g (sat 3.4g, mono 4.1g, poly 1.2g); PROTEIN 28.2g; CARB 25.6g; FIBER 6.4g; CHOL 72mg; IRON 2.7mg; SODIUM 344mg; CALC 128mg

QUICK TIP

For a speedier version, use prechopped onions and tomato, precrumbled cheese, and chopped cooked chicken breast.

Roast Chicken Salad with Peaches, Goat Cheese, and Pecans

Fresh peaches and goat cheese headline this simple no-cook salad recipe. The 8-ingredient vinaigrette, made with pantry staples, takes minutes to make and is a delicious complement to the other ingredients in the salad. Use a store-bought rotisserie chicken to save time in the kitchen. Serve with herbed bread.

Yield: 4 servings (serving size: about 1¾ cups salad and 1½ teaspoons cheese)

2½ tablespoons balsamic vinegar

1½ tablespoons extra-virgin olive oil

1½ tablespoons minced shallots

2½ teaspoons fresh lemon juice

2½ teaspoons maple syrup

¾ teaspoon Dijon mustard

¼ teaspoon kosher salt

¼ teaspoon freshly ground black pepper

2 cups shredded skinless, boneless rotisserie chicken breast

2 cups sliced peeled peaches

½ cup vertically sliced red onion

¼ cup chopped pecans, toasted

1 (5-ounce) package gourmet salad greens

2 tablespoons crumbled goat cheese

1. Combine first 8 ingredients; stir with a whisk.

2. Combine chicken and remaining ingredients except cheese in a large bowl. Add vinegar mixture; toss gently. Sprinkle with cheese.

CALORIES 285; FAT 14g (sat 2.4g, mono 7.8g, poly 2.8g); PROTEIN 24.6g; CARB 16g; FIBER 2.9g; CHOL 61mg; IRON 1.9mg; SODIUM 203mg; CALC 54mg

INGREDIENT TIP

Although we absolutely love the sweet freshness peaches add to this summertime salad,

apricots or nectarines make a good substitute, too. Just be sure to use the freshest fruits you have on hand.

Chicken and Farfalle Salad with Walnut Pesto

To make sure the walnut pesto ingredients are evenly minced, stop the food processor halfway through processing, and scrape down the sides.

Yield: 4 servings (serving size: 1½ cups salad and 1 lettuce leaf)

Salad:

2 cups uncooked farfalle (bow tie pasta; about 6 ounces)

2 cups cubed cooked skinless, boneless chicken breast

1 cup quartered cherry tomatoes

2 tablespoons chopped pitted kalamata olives

Walnut Pesto:

1 cup basil leaves

½ cup fresh parsley leaves

3 tablespoons coarsely chopped walnuts, toasted

1½ tablespoons extra-virgin olive oil

1 tablespoon white wine vinegar

½ teaspoon salt

1 garlic clove

Remaining Ingredient:

4 curly leaf lettuce leaves

1. To prepare salad, cook pasta according to package directions, omitting salt and fat. Drain; rinse with cold water. Combine pasta, chicken, tomatoes, and olives in a large bowl.

2. To prepare walnut pesto, place basil and next 6 ingredients in a food processor; pulse 6 times or until finely minced. Add pesto to pasta mixture, tossing gently to coat. Place 1 lettuce leaf on each of 4 plates; top each serving with salad mixture.

CALORIES 374; FAT 12.5g (sat 2g, mono 5.5g, poly 3.9g); PROTEIN 29.4g; CARB 36.3g; FIBER 3g; CHOL 60mg; IRON 3.6mg; SODIUM 393mg; CALC 62mg

INGREDIENT TIP

Keep kalamata olives on hand to add zesty saltiness to salads, sandwiches, and spreads.

Arugula Salad with Chicken and Apricots

This simple main course salad is perfect for lunch or a light supper option. Plums or peaches would be a delicious substitute for the apricots.

Yield: 4 servings

2 (6-ounce) skinless, boneless chicken breast halves

1 tablespoon minced fresh parsley

2 teaspoons minced fresh tarragon

½ teaspoon salt, divided

¼ teaspoon freshly ground black pepper

Cooking spray

3 tablespoons olive oil

4 teaspoons white wine vinegar

Dash of freshly ground black pepper

4 cups baby arugula

4 cups gourmet salad greens

3 apricots (about 8 ounces), pitted and thinly sliced

⅓ cup thinly vertically sliced red onion

1. Prepare grill to medium-high heat.

2. Place chicken between 2 sheets of heavy-duty plastic wrap; pound each piece to ½-inch thickness using a meat mallet or small heavy skillet. Sprinkle chicken with parsley, tarragon, ¼ teaspoon salt, and ¼ teaspoon pepper.

3. Place chicken on grill rack coated with cooking spray; grill 4 minutes on each side or until done. Transfer to a plate; cool to room temperature.

4. Combine oil, vinegar, remaining ¼ teaspoon salt, and dash of pepper in a small bowl, stirring with a whisk.

5. Combine arugula, greens, apricots, and onion in a large bowl. Pour vinaigrette over arugula mixture; toss well to coat. Place about 2 cups arugula mixture on each of 4 plates. Cut chicken breast halves crosswise into thin slices; top each serving evenly with chicken. Serve immediately.

CALORIES 243; FAT 12.9g (sat 2.1g, mono 8.3g, poly 1.7g); PROTEIN 22.2g; CARB 10.1g; FIBER 2.9g; CHOL 54mg; IRON 2.1mg; SODIUM 364mg; CALC 86mg

WINE TIP

In this salad, arugula's peppery bite is nicely balanced by fragrant herbs, sweet apricots, and grilled chicken. A pinot gris from Oregon is a great wine to serve with a complexly flavored salad like this. It has a fresh, clean feel and a creamy, fruity flavor.

Hearts of Romaine Caesar Salad with Grilled Chicken

Coddling the egg makes it creamy but does not heat it to 160°, the temperature required to kill bacteria. Use a pasteurized whole egg if you have safety concerns.

Yield: 4 servings

1 large egg

½ teaspoon freshly ground black pepper

¼ teaspoon kosher salt

2 canned anchovy fillets

2 garlic cloves

1 tablespoon fresh lemon juice

1 tablespoon extra-virgin olive oil

1 tablespoon water

1⅓ cups plain croutons

2 heads hearts of romaine lettuce, leaves separated (about 14 ounces)

3 servings Lemon-Grilled Chicken Breasts (recipe on page 71), thinly sliced

¼ cup (1 ounce) grated Parmigiano-Reggiano cheese

1. Place egg in a small bowl or coffee mug; cover with boiling water. Let stand 1 minute. Rinse egg with cold water; break egg into a small bowl.

2. Place pepper and next 3 ingredients in a mini food processor; process until minced. Add egg and juice; process 1 minute or until thick. Gradually add oil and 1 tablespoon water, processing until blended.

3. Combine croutons, lettuce, Lemon-Grilled Chicken Breasts, and egg mixture in a large bowl; toss gently. Divide salad evenly among 4 plates. Sprinkle each serving with 1 tablespoon cheese.

CALORIES 261; FAT 10.1g (sat 2.8g, mono 5.2g, poly 1.3g); PROTEIN 29.3g; CARB 12.5g; FIBER 1.8g; CHOL 115mg; IRON 2.9mg; SODIUM 561mg; CALC 165mg

Pan-Roasted Chicken, Squash, and Chard Salad with Bacon Vinaigrette

Chard is often cooked to tenderize the tough, fibrous stems. Here the crisp leaves are sliced and used as a salad green. To add interest, use a variety of seasonal wild mushrooms, such as oyster, lobster, or chanterelle. Be sure to check the temperature of the chicken breasts early because they will probably cook a little more quickly than the leg quarters.

Yield: 4 servings

Chicken:

2 bone-in chicken breast halves

2 chicken leg quarters

½ teaspoon salt

¼ teaspoon freshly ground black pepper

2 teaspoons canola oil

Salad:

1⅔ cups sliced Fuji apple

1 tablespoon fresh lemon juice

8 ounces Swiss chard leaves, thinly sliced

1 tablespoon butter

4¼ cups (¼-inch) cubed peeled butternut squash (about 1½ pounds)

¼ teaspoon salt

¼ teaspoon freshly ground black pepper, divided

3 tablespoons maple syrup

Vinaigrette:

2 bacon slices, cut crosswise into ½-inch-thick pieces

8 ounces wild mushrooms, halved

2 garlic cloves, minced

3 tablespoons apple cider vinegar

¼ cup fat-free, less-sodium chicken broth

Remaining Ingredient:

3 tablespoons walnuts, toasted and coarsely chopped

1. Preheat oven to 400°.

2. To prepare chicken, loosen skin from breast halves and leg quarters by inserting fingers, gently pushing between skin and meat. Combine ½ teaspoon salt and ¼ teaspoon black pepper; rub salt mixture evenly under loosened skin. Heat oil in a large ovenproof skillet over medium-high heat. Add chicken, skin side down, to pan; cook 5 minutes or until brown. Bake at 400° for 28 minutes or until a thermometer registers 165°. Remove chicken from pan; let stand 10 minutes. Discard skin. Place a zip-top plastic bag inside a 2-cup glass measure. Pour drippings into bag; let stand 10 minutes (fat will rise to the top). Seal bag; carefully snip off 1 bottom corner of bag. Drain drippings into a bowl, stopping before fat layer reaches opening. Reserve drippings and 2 tablespoons fat; discard remaining fat.

3. To prepare salad, combine apple, juice, and chard in a large bowl; toss to coat. Melt butter in a large skillet over medium-high heat. Add squash to pan; sprinkle with ¼ teaspoon salt and ⅛ teaspoon black pepper. Cook 10 minutes or until tender, turning to brown on all sides. Remove from heat; stir in maple syrup. Add squash mixture to apple mixture. Sprinkle salad with remaining ⅛ teaspoon black pepper; toss.

4. To prepare vinaigrette, heat reserved 2 tablespoons chicken fat in pan over medium heat. Add bacon to pan; cook 4 minutes or until crisp, stirring occasionally. Add mushrooms and garlic to bacon mixture; cook 3 minutes, stirring frequently. Stir in cider vinegar, scraping pan to loosen browned bits; cook 1 minute or until liquid evaporates. Stir in reserved chicken drippings and broth; bring to a boil. Remove from heat. Arrange 2 cups apple mixture on each of 4 plates; drizzle each serving with ¼ cup vinaigrette. Top each serving with 1 chicken breast half or 1 leg quarter, and sprinkle each serving with 2¼ teaspoons walnuts.

CALORIES 488; FAT 19.2g (sat 5.2g, mono 6.4g, poly 5.3g); PROTEIN 41.5g; CARB 40.8g; FIBER 6g; CHOL 128mg; IRON 5.1mg; SODIUM 845mg; CALC 143mg

Chicken and Bacon Roll-Ups

Made hearty with shredded chicken, these easy sandwiches can be endlessly adapted to suit any taste. Add sweet potato chips to complete the meal.

Yield: 4 servings (serving size: 1 wrap)

½ cup reduced-fat mayonnaise

1 teaspoon minced fresh tarragon

2 teaspoons fresh lemon juice

4 (2.8-ounce) whole wheat flatbreads (such as Flatout)

2 cups shredded romaine lettuce

2 cups chopped tomato (about 2 medium)

4 center-cut bacon slices, cooked and drained

2 cups shredded skinless, boneless rotisserie chicken breast

1. Combine reduced-fat mayonnaise, minced tarragon, and fresh lemon juice in a small bowl. Spread 2 tablespoons mayonnaise mixture over each flatbread. Top each with ½ cup shredded romaine lettuce, ½ cup chopped tomato, 1 bacon slice, crumbled, and ½ cup chicken. Roll up.

CALORIES 433; FAT 13g (sat 2.6g, mono 2g, poly 0.9g); PROTEIN 34.8g; CARB 44.2g; FIBER 5.5g; CHOL 66mg; IRON 3.1mg; SODIUM 925mg; CALC 49mg

FLAVOR TIP

Substitute 1 teaspoon chopped fresh basil or chives for tarragon in the mayonnaise mixture, if you prefer. Also, use flavored wraps, or try applewood-smoked bacon for a smoky punch.

Mediterranean Chicken Salad Pitas

Add honeydew melon and cantaloupe slices on the side to complete your meal.

Yield: 6 servings (serving size: 2 stuffed pita halves)

1 cup plain whole-milk Greek yogurt (such as Fage Total Classic)

2 tablespoons lemon juice

½ teaspoon ground cumin

¼ teaspoon crushed red pepper

3 cups chopped cooked chicken

1 cup chopped red bell pepper (about 1 large)

½ cup chopped pitted green olives (about 20 small)

½ cup diced red onion

¼ cup chopped fresh cilantro

1 (15-ounce) can no-salt-added chickpeas (garbanzo beans), rinsed and drained

6 (6-inch) whole wheat pitas, cut in half

12 Bibb lettuce leaves

6 (⅛-inch-thick) slices tomato, cut in half

1. Combine first 4 ingredients in a small bowl; set aside. Combine chicken and next 5 ingredients in a large bowl. Add yogurt mixture to chicken mixture; toss gently to coat. Line each pita half with 1 lettuce leaf and 1 tomato piece; add ½ cup chicken mixture to each pita half.

CALORIES 404; FAT 10.2g (sat 3.8g, mono 4g, poly 1.5g); PROTEIN 33.6g; CARB 46.4g; FIBER 6g; CHOL 66mg; IRON 3.4mg; SODIUM 575mg; CALC 110mg

INGREDIENT TIP

Greek yogurt has a thick, rich consistency similar to sour cream. It gives the pita filling a creamy texture.

Little Italy Chicken Pitas with Sun-Dried Tomato Vinaigrette

Use oil from the sun-dried tomatoes to prepare the vinaigrette for this zesty sandwich. Chilled green grapes make a cool side addition.

Yield: 6 servings (serving size: 2 stuffed pita halves)

2 tablespoons balsamic vinegar

1½ tablespoons sun-dried tomato oil

1 tablespoon chopped drained oil-packed sun-dried tomatoes

¼ teaspoon freshly ground black pepper

1 garlic clove, minced

4 cups shredded cooked chicken breast (about ¾ pound)

1 cup chopped tomato (about 1 medium)

½ cup (2 ounces) grated Asiago cheese

¼ cup thinly sliced fresh basil

6 (6-inch) pitas, cut in half

3 cups mixed baby greens

1. Combine first 5 ingredients in a large bowl. Stir in chicken, tomato, cheese, and basil. Line each pita half with ¼ cup greens. Divide chicken mixture evenly among pita halves.

CALORIES 342; FAT 9.1g (sat 2.8g, mono 4.2g, poly 1.3g); PROTEIN 26.4g; CARB 37.3g; FIBER 2.4g; CHOL 56mg; IRON 2.7mg; SODIUM 397mg; CALC 162mg

Rosemary Chicken Salad Sandwiches

Although this seems like your typical chicken and mayonnaise mixture, crunchy smoked almonds, fresh rosemary, green onions, and a little Dijon mustard make this anything but ordinary. Add a lettuce leaf to each sandwich, if desired.

Yield: 5 servings (serving size: 1 sandwich)

3 cups chopped roasted skinless, boneless chicken breast (about ¾ pound)

⅓ cup chopped green onions

¼ cup chopped smoked almonds

¼ cup plain fat-free yogurt

¼ cup light mayonnaise

1 teaspoon chopped fresh rosemary

1 teaspoon Dijon mustard

⅛ teaspoon salt

⅛ teaspoon freshly ground black pepper

10 slices whole-grain bread

1. Combine first 9 ingredients, stirring well. Spread about ⅔ cup chicken mixture over each of 5 bread slices, and top with remaining bread slices. Cut sandwiches diagonally in half.

CALORIES 360; FAT 11.6g (sat 2.1g, mono 3.5g, poly 1.8g); PROTEIN 33.6g; CARB 29.9g; FIBER 4.4g; CHOL 76mg; IRON 2.9mg; SODIUM 529mg; CALC 104mg

Skillet Chicken Souvlaki

Prepare a family-friendly Mediterranean-style dish that's sure to please even the pickiest eater. The quick-cooking chicken and simple homemade yogurt sauce make this a perfect dish for a busy weeknight. Serve with a simple side salad.

Yield: 4 servings (serving size: 1 cup chicken mixture, ¼ cup sauce, 1 pita, and about ¼ cup tomato slices)

1 tablespoon olive oil, divided

1 pound skinless, boneless chicken breast, thinly sliced

½ teaspoon salt

¼ teaspoon freshly ground black pepper

1½ cups vertically sliced onion (about 1 medium)

1 cup thinly sliced green bell pepper (about 1)

2 teaspoons bottled minced garlic

½ teaspoon dried oregano

½ cup grated English cucumber

¼ cup 2% Greek-style yogurt (such as Fage)

¼ cup reduced-fat sour cream

1 tablespoon chopped fresh flat-leaf parsley

½ teaspoon grated lemon rind

1 teaspoon fresh lemon juice

⅛ teaspoon salt

4 (6-inch) whole wheat soft pitas, cut in half and warmed

2 plum tomatoes, thinly sliced

1. Heat 2 teaspoons oil in a large nonstick skillet over medium-high heat. Sprinkle chicken with ½ teaspoon salt and black pepper. Add chicken to pan; sauté 5 minutes or until done. Remove from pan.

2. Add 1 teaspoon oil to pan. Add onion and bell pepper; sauté 3 minutes. Add chicken, garlic, and oregano; cook 30 seconds.

3. Combine cucumber and next 6 ingredients. Serve chicken mixture with yogurt sauce, warmed pita, and tomato slices.

CALORIES 361; FAT 7.4g (sat 2.3g, mono 3.3g, poly 0.8g); PROTEIN 35.1g; CARB 39g; FIBER 4.7g; CHOL 72mg; IRON 3.1mg; SODIUM 589mg; CALC 105mg

QUICK TIP

To quickly vertically slice an onion, start at the end opposite the root. Slice the top off the onion, leaving the root intact. Remove the papery skin, and slice the onion vertically. Continue cutting the onion vertically into thin slices.

Mozzarella Chicken Sandwich

This sandwich provides two grain servings from the ciabatta, a little more than two servings of meat from the chicken, and half a dairy serving from the cheese. Serve with orange wedges and baked chips.

Yield: 4 servings (serving size: 1 sandwich)

¼ cup (about 2 ounces) sun-dried tomato pesto (such as Classico)

2 tablespoons fat-free mayonnaise

¾ pound skinless, boneless chicken breasts

¼ teaspoon pepper

⅛ teaspoon salt

1 teaspoon olive oil

1 (8-ounce) loaf ciabatta

12 large fresh basil leaves

¾ cup (3 ounces) shredded part-skim mozzarella cheese

½ cup sliced bottled roasted red bell peppers

1 large tomato, thinly sliced

1. Combine pesto and mayonnaise in a small bowl, stirring to blend.
2. Sprinkle chicken with pepper and salt. Heat oil in a large nonstick skillet over medium-high heat. Add chicken, and cook 3 minutes on each side or until done. Remove chicken to a cutting board, and cool slightly. Cut chicken lengthwise into thin slices.
3. Preheat broiler.
4. Cut ciabatta in half horizontally. Place bread, cut sides up, on a baking sheet. Broil 3 minutes or until lightly browned. Remove bread from pan. Spread pesto mixture evenly over cut sides of bread. Arrange chicken slices evenly over bottom half. Top chicken evenly with basil leaves, and sprinkle cheese over top. Place bottom half on baking sheet, and broil 2 minutes or until cheese melts. Arrange bell pepper and tomato over cheese, and cover with top half of bread. Cut into 4 equal pieces.

CALORIES 394; FAT 13.4g (sat 3.9g, mono 7.4g, poly 1.1g); PROTEIN 31.3g; CARB 37.3g; FIBER 2g; CHOL 63mg; IRON 2.8mg; SODIUM 796mg; CALC 187mg

Honey-Chipotle Barbecue Chicken Sandwiches

This recipe yields slow-cooked barbecue flavor in less than an hour. Broil the sandwiches just before serving.

Yield: 4 sandwiches (serving size: 1 sandwich)

½ cup water

1 teaspoon ground cumin

4 garlic cloves, thinly sliced

1 pound skinless, boneless chicken breast

1 (7-ounce) can chipotle chiles in adobo sauce

1 tablespoon canola oil

1 tablespoon minced garlic

1 teaspoon ground cumin

½ cup canned tomato puree

¼ cup cider vinegar

3 tablespoons honey

1 tablespoon Worcestershire sauce

¼ teaspoon salt

4 (1½-ounce) sandwich rolls

2 ounces Monterey Jack cheese, thinly sliced

4 (⅛-inch-thick) slices red onion

1. Combine water, 1 teaspoon cumin, 4 sliced garlic cloves, and chicken in a large saucepan. Cover and bring to a boil over medium-high heat. Reduce heat to medium-low; cook 10 minutes or until chicken is done. Drain, and place chicken on a cutting board. Cut chicken across grain into thin slices; keep warm.

2. Remove 2 tablespoons adobo sauce from can; set aside. Remove 2 chipotle chiles from can; finely chop and set aside. Reserve remaining chiles and adobo sauce for another use.

3. Heat oil in a large nonstick skillet over medium-high heat. Add 1 tablespoon minced garlic; sauté 3 minutes or until just beginning to brown. Add 1 teaspoon cumin; sauté 1 minute. Stir in tomato puree; cook 4 minutes or until mixture thickens to a pastelike consistency, stirring constantly. Stir in reserved 2 tablespoons adobo sauce, 2 chopped chipotle chiles, vinegar, honey, Worcestershire, and ¼ teaspoon salt. Add sliced chicken to sauce; simmer for 3 minutes or until thoroughly heated.

4. Preheat broiler.

5. Split rolls in half; arrange in a single layer, cut sides up, on a baking sheet. Broil 1 minute or until lightly toasted. Remove top halves of rolls from baking sheet. Divide chicken mixture evenly among bottom halves of rolls, and top chicken mixture evenly with cheese. Broil chicken-topped rolls 2 minutes or until cheese melts. Remove from oven; top with onion and top roll halves. Serve immediately.

CALORIES 424; FAT 11.8g (sat 3.9g, mono 4.7g, poly 1.9g); PROTEIN 34.5g; CARB 45.1g; FIBER 2.6g; CHOL 78mg; IRON 3.6mg; SODIUM 765mg; CALC 211mg

Chicken and Roquefort Sandwiches

One serving of this entrée contains about one-fourth of your daily sodium allotment. We extend salty Roquefort cheese by mixing it with cream cheese as a spread. A 2-ounce portion size for bread also helps control sodium counts.

Yield: 4 servings (serving size: 1 sandwich)

½ cup (about 3 ounces) tub whipped cream cheese

¼ cup (1 ounce) crumbled blue cheese

2 tablespoons finely chopped celery

1½ teaspoons chopped fresh chives

2 teaspoons olive oil

2 (6-ounce) skinless, boneless chicken breast halves

¼ teaspoon coarsely ground black pepper

⅛ teaspoon salt

1 (8-ounce) baguette

2 small heirloom tomatoes, thinly sliced (about 8 ounces)

½ cup baby arugula leaves

1. Combine first 4 ingredients in a bowl.

2. Heat oil in a nonstick skillet over medium-high heat. Sprinkle chicken with pepper. Add chicken to pan; cook 5 minutes on each side or until chicken is done. Remove from heat, and let stand 5 minutes. Cut lengthwise into ⅓-inch-thick strips. Sprinkle evenly with ⅛ teaspoon salt.

3. Cut baguette in half lengthwise. Spread cheese mixture over cut sides of baguette. Arrange chicken, tomato slices, and arugula evenly over bottom half of baguette; cover with top half. Cut crosswise into 4 equal pieces.

CALORIES 392; FAT 15.8g (sat 7g, mono 5.2g, poly 1.2g); PROTEIN 27.9g; CARB 35.1g; FIBER 2.2g; CHOL 84mg; IRON 3.1mg; SODIUM 640mg; CALC 100mg

WINE TIP

The dramatic, salty flavor of blue cheese is the main consideration in matching this sandwich to wine. A crisp, light, dry riesling has the right fruitiness to counteract those salty notes.

Spicy Chicken Sandwiches with Cilantro-Lime Mayo

Chicken cutlets are encrusted with tortilla chip crumbs, which yield a satisfying crunch. You can also use spicy chips for more heat.

Yield: 4 servings (serving size: 1 sandwich)

Mayo:

¼ cup reduced-fat mayonnaise

2 tablespoons chopped fresh cilantro

1 teaspoon fresh lime juice

1 garlic clove, minced

Chicken:

¼ cup egg substitute

3 tablespoons hot sauce (such as Tabasco)

1 teaspoon dried oregano

½ teaspoon salt

2 (6-ounce) skinless, boneless chicken breast halves

4½ ounces baked tortilla chips (about 6 cups)

2 tablespoons olive oil

Remaining Ingredients:

4 (2-ounce) Kaiser rolls, split

12 (⅛-inch-thick) slices red onion

4 lettuce leaves

1. To prepare mayo, combine first 4 ingredients; refrigerate until ready to prepare sandwiches.

2. To prepare chicken, combine egg substitute, hot sauce, oregano, and salt in a large zip-top plastic bag. Cut chicken breast halves in half horizontally to form 4 cutlets. Add chicken to bag; seal. Marinate in refrigerator 2 hours or up to 8 hours, turning bag occasionally.

3. Place tortilla chips in a food processor; process 1 minute or until ground. Place ground chips in a shallow dish.

4. Working with one cutlet at a time, remove chicken from marinade, allowing excess to drip off. Coat chicken completely in chips. Set aside. Repeat procedure with remaining chicken and chips.

5. Heat a large nonstick skillet over medium heat. Add olive oil to pan, swirling to coat. Add chicken to pan; cook 3 minutes on each side or until browned and done. Spread mayo evenly over cut sides of rolls. Layer bottom half of each roll with 3 onion slices, 1 lettuce leaf, and 1 chicken cutlet; top with top halves of rolls.

CALORIES 419; FAT 13.2g (sat 1.7g, mono 6.1g, poly 3.4g); PROTEIN 28.1g; CARB 46.8g; FIBER 2.6g; CHOL 49mg; IRON 3.2mg; SODIUM 759mg; CALC 101mg

BBQ Chicken Pizza

Online reviews raved about the contrast of flavors provided by tangy tomato chutney, savory chicken, and sharp cheddar cheese. If you can't find tomato chutney, make your own (see note below), or use store-bought barbecue sauce.

Yield: 6 servings (serving size: 1 wedge)

1 (10-ounce) Italian cheese-flavored thin pizza crust (such as Boboli)

¾ cup tomato chutney

2 cups chopped roasted skinless, boneless chicken breast (about 2 breasts)

⅔ cup diced plum tomato

¾ cup (3 ounces) shredded extra-sharp white cheddar cheese

⅓ cup chopped green onions

1. Preheat oven to 450°.
2. Place crust on a baking sheet. Bake at 450° for 3 minutes. Remove from oven; spread chutney over crust, leaving a ½-inch border.
3. Top chutney with chicken. Sprinkle diced tomato, cheese, and green onions evenly over chicken. Bake at 450° for 9 minutes or until cheese melts. Cut pizza into 6 wedges.
Note: If you can't find tomato chutney, make your own. Combine 2 cups diced plum tomato, 3 tablespoons brown sugar, 3 tablespoons cider vinegar, ⅛ teaspoon Jamaican jerk seasoning, and 1 minced garlic clove in a small saucepan; bring to a boil. Reduce heat to medium; cook 20 minutes or until thickened.

CALORIES 300; FAT 8.5g (sat 3.9g, mono 2.9g, poly 1g); PROTEIN 21.3g; CARB 35.2g; FIBER 1.2g; CHOL 48mg; IRON 1.7mg; SODIUM 622mg; CALC 247mg

QUICK TIP

We've used a Boboli crust here to speed up the preparation time. It's a great alternative to making and baking your own crust.

Cuban Chicken Pizza

Flour tortillas pinch-hit as a crisp crust for this hearty pizza loaded with chicken and vegetables. Toasting the corn in a skillet brings out its natural sweetness and adds a deliciously smoky note.

Yield: 4 servings (serving size: 1 pizza)

4 (8-inch) fat-free flour tortillas

Cooking spray

1 (11-ounce) can no-salt-added whole-kernel corn, drained

½ teaspoon cumin seeds

2 cups diced roasted chicken breast

1 (15-ounce) can black beans, rinsed and drained

1 garlic clove, minced

2 tablespoons fresh lime juice

¾ cup Monterey Jack cheese with jalapeño peppers

4 teaspoons chopped fresh cilantro

1. Preheat oven to 350°.

2. Place flour tortillas on a baking sheet coated with cooking spray. Bake at 350° for 10 minutes or until edges are light brown. Remove from oven; stack and press down to flatten. Set aside.

3. Heat a large nonstick skillet over medium-high heat; coat pan with cooking spray. Add corn to pan, and cook 1 minute or until lightly charred. Add cumin seeds; cook 5 seconds, stirring constantly. Add chicken, black beans, and garlic; cook 2 minutes or until thoroughly heated. Remove from heat; stir in lime juice.

4. Place tortillas on baking sheet. Spoon ¾ cup bean mixture onto each tortilla; top each with 3 tablespoons cheese. Bake at 350° for 2 minutes or until the cheese melts. Sprinkle each pizza with 1 teaspoon cilantro.

CALORIES 460; FAT 10.2g (sat 4.8g, mono 2.9g, poly 1.7g); PROTEIN 37.7g; CARB 54.3g; FIBER 8.4g; CHOL 78mg; IRON 3.6mg; SODIUM 760mg; CALC 210mg

Ratatouille Pizza with Chicken

The addition of chicken to a quick ratatouille makes a great-tasting and satisfying pizza when put on a crust. Serve with a green salad for a light weekday supper.

Yield: 6 servings

1 teaspoon olive oil

1 Japanese eggplant, halved lengthwise and cut into (¼-inch-thick) slices

1 red bell pepper, cut into ¼-inch strips

½ small red onion, thinly sliced

1 cup sliced mushrooms

¾ teaspoon dried Italian seasoning

¼ teaspoon salt

4 garlic cloves, minced

1 (10-ounce) Italian cheese-flavored thin pizza crust (such as Boboli)

1 cup chopped skinless, boneless rotisserie chicken breast

1 cup (4 ounces) preshredded reduced-fat pizza-blend cheese

3 plum tomatoes, cut into (¼-inch-thick) slices

Cooking spray

3 tablespoons finely chopped fresh flat-leaf parsley

1. Preheat oven to 375°.

2. Heat a large nonstick skillet over medium-high heat. Add oil to pan. Add eggplant, bell pepper, and onion; sauté 3 minutes or until eggplant begins to soften. Reduce heat to medium. Add mushrooms; cook 3 minutes, stirring frequently. Add Italian seasoning, salt, and garlic; cook 1 minute, stirring constantly. Remove from heat.

3. Place crust on a baking sheet. Spread vegetable mixture evenly over crust, leaving a ½-inch border. Arrange chicken over vegetable mixture; sprinkle evenly with cheese. Arrange tomatoes over cheese, and lightly coat with cooking spray. Bake at 375° for 25 minutes or until cheese is bubbly and tomatoes are softened. Sprinkle with parsley.

CALORIES 249; FAT 8.3g (sat 3.9g, mono 2g, poly 0.8g); PROTEIN 18.1g; CARB 26.3g; FIBER 1.8g; CHOL 33mg; IRON 2mg; SODIUM 409mg; CALC 273mg

soups
& stews

Broccoli and Chicken Noodle Soup

Count on having dinner on the table in about 40 minutes, and serve this soup the moment it's done for the best results. In fact, if you wait, you'll find it gets too thick with time. If you have leftovers, you will want to thin the soup with a little chicken broth or milk to the desired consistency.

Yield: 10 servings (serving size: 1 cup)

Cooking spray

2 cups chopped onion

1 cup presliced mushrooms

1 garlic clove, minced

3 tablespoons butter

1.1 ounces all-purpose flour (about ¼ cup)

4 cups 1% low-fat milk

1 (14-ounce) can fat-free, less-sodium chicken broth

4 ounces uncooked vermicelli, broken into 2-inch pieces

2 cups (8 ounces) shredded light processed cheese (such as Velveeta Light)

4 cups (1-inch) cubed cooked chicken breast

3 cups small broccoli florets (8 ounces)

1 cup half-and-half

1 teaspoon freshly ground black pepper

¾ teaspoon salt

1. Heat a Dutch oven over medium-high heat. Coat pan with cooking spray. Add onion, mushrooms, and garlic to pan; sauté 5 minutes or until liquid evaporates, stirring occasionally. Reduce heat to medium; add butter to mushroom mixture, stirring until butter melts. Sprinkle mushroom mixture with flour; cook 2 minutes, stirring occasionally. Gradually add milk and broth, stirring constantly with a whisk; bring to a boil. Reduce heat to medium-low cook 10 minutes or until slightly thick, stirring constantly. Add pasta to pan, and cook 10 minutes. Add cheese to pan, and stir until cheese melts. Add chicken and remaining ingredients to pan; cook 5 minutes or until broccoli is tender and soup is thoroughly heated.

CALORIES 317; FAT 12.3g (sat 6.8g, mono 2.9g, poly 0.9g); PROTEIN 27.5g; CARB 23.8g; FIBER 1.9g; CHOL 74mg; IRON 1.6mg; SODIUM 723mg; CALC 179mg

QUICK TIP

If the broccoli florets are large, break them into smaller pieces at the stalk instead of chopping them; they'll cook more quickly.

Chicken-Escarole Soup

To cut down on prep time and keep cleanup to a minimum, use kitchen shears to easily chop tomatoes while they're still in the can.

Yield: 4 servings (serving size: 1 cup)

1 (14½-ounce) can Italian-style stewed tomatoes, undrained and chopped

1 (14-ounce) can fat-free, less-sodium chicken broth

1 cup chopped cooked chicken breast

2 cups coarsely chopped escarole (about 1 small head)

2 teaspoons extra-virgin olive oil

1. Combine tomatoes and broth in a large saucepan. Cover and bring to a boil over high heat. Reduce heat to low; simmer 5 minutes. Add chicken, escarole, and oil; cook 5 minutes.

CALORIES 118; FAT 4g (sat 0.7g, mono 2.1g, poly 0.6g); PROTEIN 13.5g; CARB 7.9g; FIBER 1.5g; CHOL 30mg; IRON 1.1mg; SODIUM 535mg; CALC 49mg

INGREDIENT TIP

Escarole is a variety of endive but is not as bitter as Belgian endive or curly endive. It has broad, bright green leaves that grow in loose

heads. When purchasing escarole, look for fresh, crisp leaves without discoloration. Store escarole tightly wrapped in the refrigerator for up to three days.

Chicken-Vegetable Soup

Americans of Eastern European heritage add a variety of root vegetables, such as turnips and parsnips, to chicken soup for subtle sweetness and bite. Feel free to omit them and simply add more carrot and leek, if you prefer. Be sure to cook the egg noodles separately so the starch in the noodles doesn't cloud the clear soup broth.

Yield: 8 servings

1 (6-pound) roasting chicken

8 cups water

2½ cups chopped celery (about 4 stalks)

2 cups thinly sliced leek (about 2 large)

1½ cups (½-inch) cubed parsnip (about 8 ounces)

1½ cups (½-inch) cubed carrot (about 8 ounces)

1½ cups (½-inch) cubed turnip (about 8 ounces)

1 teaspoon kosher salt

½ teaspoon freshly ground black pepper

1 teaspoon chopped fresh dill (optional)

8 ounces egg noodles

1. Remove and discard giblets and neck from chicken. Remove and discard skin from chicken; trim excess fat. Split chicken in half lengthwise; place in a Dutch oven. Cover with 8 cups water; bring to a boil. Cook 10 minutes. Skim fat from surface of broth; discard fat. Add celery and next 4 ingredients to pan, stirring well; bring to a boil. Reduce heat, and simmer 30 minutes or until vegetables are almost tender, stirring occasionally. Remove chicken; let stand 10 minutes. Remove chicken from bones; shred chicken with 2 forks to yield 6 cups meat. Discard bones. Simmer vegetable mixture 10 minutes or until tender. Return shredded chicken to pan. Stir in salt, pepper, and dill, if desired.

2. Cook noodles according to package directions, omitting salt and fat. Place ½ cup noodles in each of 8 bowls; top each serving with 1½ cups chicken mixture.

CALORIES 404; FAT 14.2g (sat 3.6g, mono 4.7g, poly 3.5g); PROTEIN 36.5g; CARB 31.2g; FIBER 3.6g; CHOL 107mg; IRON 3.4mg; SODIUM 392mg; CALC 76mg

Roasted Vegetable–Rosemary Chicken Soup

This hearty soup's flavor comes from the roasted vegetables that have been caramelized. Serve with crusty bread on a cold winter's night.

Yield: 8 servings (serving size: about 1 cup)

1 cup (1-inch) cubed carrot

1 cup (1-inch) cubed onion

1 cup coarsely chopped mushrooms

1 cup (1-inch) pieces celery

1 cup (1-inch) pieces red bell pepper

2 tablespoons extra-virgin olive oil

1 cup water

2 tablespoons chopped fresh rosemary

¼ teaspoon salt

4 (14-ounce) cans fat-free, less-sodium chicken broth

2 garlic cloves, minced

1 pound skinless, boneless chicken breast, cut into ½-inch pieces

2 cups uncooked whole wheat rotini (corkscrew pasta)

Rosemary sprigs (optional)

1. Preheat oven to 375°.

2. Combine first 5 ingredients in a large bowl; drizzle with oil, and toss well to coat. Arrange vegetable mixture in a single layer on a jelly-roll pan lined with foil. Bake at 375° for 50 minutes or until browned, stirring occasionally.

3. Combine water and next 5 ingredients in a large Dutch oven; bring to a boil. Reduce heat, and simmer 30 minutes. Add roasted vegetables; simmer 30 minutes. Bring soup to a boil. Add pasta; simmer 10 minutes, stirring occasionally. Ladle soup into individual bowls, and garnish with rosemary sprigs, if desired.

CALORIES 176; FAT 4.8g (sat 0.8g, mono 3g, poly 0.7g); PROTEIN 17.9g; CARB 15.5g; FIBER 2.3g; CHOL 33mg; IRON 1.5mg; SODIUM 450mg; CALC 45mg

Tuscan Chicken Soup

This recipe uses many common pantry staples and refrigerator ingredients. All you have to do is pick up fresh spinach and chicken thighs at the supermarket.

Yield: 4 servings

1 cup chopped onion

2 tablespoons tomato paste

¼ teaspoon salt

¼ teaspoon freshly ground black pepper

1 (15-ounce) can cannellini beans, rinsed and drained

1 (14-ounce) can fat-free, less-sodium chicken broth

1 (7-ounce) bottle roasted red bell peppers, rinsed, drained, and cut into ½-inch pieces

1 pound skinless, boneless chicken thighs, cut into 1-inch pieces

3 garlic cloves, minced

½ teaspoon chopped fresh rosemary

1 (6-ounce) package fresh baby spinach

8 teaspoons grated Parmesan cheese

1. Combine first 9 ingredients in an electric slow cooker. Cover and cook on HIGH 1 hour; reduce heat to LOW, and cook an additional 3 hours. Stir in rosemary and spinach; cook on LOW 10 minutes. Ladle 1½ cups soup into each of 4 shallow bowls; top each serving with 2 teaspoons Parmesan cheese.

CALORIES 239; FAT 5.8g (sat 1.8g, mono 1.7g, poly 1.4g); PROTEIN 28.6g; CARB 16.3g; FIBER 4.6g; CHOL 97mg; IRON 3.9mg; SODIUM 768mg; CALC 126mg

Southwestern Chicken and White Bean Soup

Here's a soup that's super quick and easy—not to mention inexpensive—and one that you will make again and again. It has a wonderful comfort-food quality that the whole family will love.

Yield: 6 servings (serving size: 1 cup)

2 cups shredded cooked chicken breast

1 tablespoon 40%-less-sodium taco seasoning (such as Old El Paso)

Cooking spray

2 (14-ounce) cans fat-free, less-sodium chicken broth

1 (16-ounce) can cannellini beans or other white beans, rinsed and drained

½ cup green salsa

Light sour cream (optional)

Chopped fresh cilantro (optional)

1. Combine chicken and taco seasoning; toss well to coat. Heat a large saucepan over medium-high heat. Coat pan with cooking spray. Add chicken; sauté 2 minutes or until chicken is lightly browned. Add broth, scraping pan to loosen browned bits.

2. Place beans in a small bowl; mash until only a few whole beans remain. Add beans and salsa to pan, stirring well. Bring to a boil. Reduce heat; simmer 10 minutes or until slightly thick. Serve with sour cream and cilantro, if desired.

CALORIES 134; FAT 3g (sat 0.5g, mono 0.6g, poly 0.5g); PROTEIN 18g; CARB 8.5g; FIBER 1.8g; CHOL 40mg; IRON 1.1mg; SODIUM 623mg; CALC 22mg

INGREDIENT TIP

We really like the extra zing of flavor from the fresh cilantro. It adds a nice burst of color to the dish as well. Simply toss some of the distinctive herb on top of the soup just before serving.

Chicken-Barley Soup with Walnut Pesto

Habanero peppers are fiery hot, so handle them carefully. In this dish, you simply pierce the chile with a fork and float it in the broth as the soup cooks. Remove it with a slotted spoon before serving. If you prefer milder heat, use the same technique with a jalapeño.

Yield: 8 servings (serving size: 1¾ cups soup and 2 tablespoons pesto)

Soup:

5 bacon slices, chopped

1½ cups chopped onion

2 tablespoons minced fresh garlic

2 (4-inch) portobello mushroom caps, chopped

1 (3-pound) whole chicken, skinned

1 fresh thyme sprig

4½ quarts cold water

8 ounces Swiss chard

1 cup uncooked pearl barley, rinsed and drained

1 cup (½-inch) cubed peeled butternut squash

½ cup finely chopped carrot

½ cup finely chopped celery

¼ cup finely chopped Granny Smith apple

1 habanero pepper

¾ teaspoon salt

¼ teaspoon freshly ground black pepper

Pesto:

¼ cup walnuts, toasted

¼ cup (1 ounce) freshly grated Parmigiano-Reggiano cheese

2 tablespoons extra-virgin olive oil

1 tablespoon minced fresh garlic

¼ teaspoon salt

1. To prepare soup, cook bacon in a large skillet over medium heat until crisp. Add onion, garlic, and mushrooms to pan; cook 5 minutes, stirring frequently. Set aside.

2. Remove and discard giblets and neck from chicken. Place chicken and thyme in a large Dutch oven over medium heat. Cover with 4½ quarts cold water; bring to a simmer. Skim fat from surface; discard. Remove stems and center ribs from Swiss chard. Coarsely chop stems and ribs; reserve leaves. Add stems, ribs, and next 5 ingredients to pan; bring to a simmer. Pierce habanero with a fork; add to pan. Cook 35 minutes or until chicken is done.

3. Remove chicken from pan; cool slightly. Remove chicken from bones; chop meat. Discard bones, thyme sprig, and habanero. Strain barley mixture through a sieve over a bowl. Reserve 4 cups of broth for another use. Return remaining 6 cups broth to pan; bring to a boil. Cook 10 minutes. Return chicken and barley mixture to pan; bring to a simmer. Add mushroom mixture. Cook 2 minutes or until thoroughly heated. Stir in ¾ teaspoon salt and ¼ teaspoon black pepper.

4. To prepare pesto, cook Swiss chard leaves in boiling water 2 minutes. Drain and rinse under cold water; drain. Place leaves, walnuts, and remaining ingredients in a food processor; process until smooth. Serve with soup.

CALORIES 416; FAT 13.7g (sat 3.1g, mono 5.6g, poly 3.7g); PROTEIN 41.8g; CARB 31.7g; FIBER 6.6g; CHOL 117mg; IRON 3.5mg; SODIUM 641mg; CALC 78mg

Chicken and Wild Rice Soup

Light cheese and a flour-and-milk mixture keep this soup creamy but surprisingly low in fat. Make a batch and reheat throughout the week for effortless and satisfying meals.

Yield: 8 servings (serving size: 1¼ cups)

1 cup uncooked quick-cooking wild rice

Cooking spray

1 cup chopped onion

2 garlic cloves, minced

3 cups fat-free, less-sodium chicken broth

1½ cups cubed peeled baking potato

3 cups 2% reduced-fat milk

1.5 ounces all-purpose flour (about ⅓ cup)

10 ounces light processed cheese, cubed (such as Velveeta Light)

2 cups chopped roasted skinless, boneless chicken breast (about 2 breasts)

½ teaspoon freshly ground black pepper

¼ teaspoon salt

¼ cup chopped fresh parsley (optional)

1. Cook rice according to package directions, omitting salt and fat.

2. Heat a large Dutch oven over medium-high heat. Coat pan with cooking spray. Add onion and garlic; sauté 3 minutes. Add broth and potato; bring to a boil over medium-high heat. Cover, reduce heat, and simmer 5 minutes or until potato is tender.

3. Combine milk and flour, stirring well with a whisk. Add milk mixture to potato mixture; cook 5 minutes or until slightly thick, stirring constantly. Remove from heat; add cheese, stirring until cheese melts. Stir in rice, chicken, pepper, and salt. Garnish with parsley, if desired.

CALORIES 280; FAT 7g (sat 4g, mono 1g, poly 0.5g); PROTEIN 24.9g; CARB 28.7g; FIBER 1.6g; CHOL 52mg; IRON 1.1mg; SODIUM 879mg; CALC 329mg

Chicken Pasta Soup

This quick twist on classic chicken noodle soup is loaded with fresh vegetables—carrots, celery, onion, and green bell pepper. You'll agree 100 percent that fresh is best.

Yield: 6 servings (serving size: 1½ cups)

Cooking spray

2 (6-ounce) skinless, boneless chicken breasts, cut into bite-sized pieces

1 (8-ounce) container refrigerated prechopped celery, onion, and bell pepper mix

1 cup matchstick-cut carrots

¼ teaspoon freshly ground black pepper

7 cups fat-free, less-sodium chicken broth

1 cup uncooked whole wheat rotini (corkscrew pasta)

1. Heat a Dutch oven over medium-high heat. Coat pan with cooking spray. Add chicken and next 3 ingredients; cook 6 minutes or until chicken begins to brown and vegetables are tender, stirring frequently. Add broth; bring to a boil. Add pasta, reduce heat to medium, and cook 8 minutes or until pasta is done.

CALORIES 156; FAT 3g (sat 0.6g, mono 0.6g, poly 0.4g); PROTEIN 20.4g; CARB 12.8g; FIBER 2.8g; CHOL 40mg; IRON 1.4mg; SODIUM 723mg; CALC 27mg

Chicken-Orzo Soup

Nothing says comfort food like a bowl of hearty chicken soup. Pair with a sandwich for a simple, heartwarming dinner option.

Yield: 4 servings (serving size: about 1½ cups)

1 (32-ounce) container fat-free, less-sodium chicken broth, divided

½ cup uncooked orzo

2 teaspoons olive oil

⅔ cup coarsely chopped carrot

½ cup coarsely chopped celery

½ cup chopped onion

¾ pound skinless, boneless chicken breast, cut into ½-inch cubes

1¼ cups water

3 fresh parsley sprigs

1 fresh thyme sprig

4 cups fresh baby spinach

1 tablespoon fresh lemon juice

¼ teaspoon salt

⅛ teaspoon black pepper

1. Bring 1¾ cups broth to a boil in a medium saucepan. Add orzo; cook 10 minutes or until done. Drain.

2. While orzo cooks, heat a large saucepan over medium heat. Add oil to pan; swirl to coat. Add carrot, celery, onion, and chicken; cook 3 minutes, stirring constantly. Stir in remaining 2¼ cups broth, 1¼ cups water, parsley, and thyme; bring to a boil. Reduce heat; cover and simmer 10 minutes or until vegetables are tender. Discard herb sprigs. Add orzo, spinach, juice, salt, and pepper; simmer 1 minute.

CALORIES 224; FAT 4.7g (sat 0.9g, mono 2.3g, poly 0.7g); PROTEIN 22g; CARB 22.6g; FIBER 3g; CHOL 47mg; IRON 1.5mg; SODIUM 750mg; CALC 43mg

Tex-Mex Chicken Tortilla Soup

Tortillas are the basis of countless Mexican dishes, such as tacos, enchiladas, and burritos, as well as our peppy Tex-Mex soup. The crunchy texture of the tortilla chips provides the perfect contrast to this fiesta-in-a-bowl, which features bright colors, bold flavors, robust spices, and sour cream and cilantro garnishes. Don't throw away any leftover tortillas; they're also ideal toasted and sprinkled over salads or casseroles.

Yield: 5 servings (serving size: 1½ cups soup, 1 tablespoon sour cream, and about 3 tortilla chips)

1 tablespoon olive oil

2 (6-ounce) skinless, boneless chicken breast halves, cut into ½-inch pieces

2 (4-ounce) skinless, boneless chicken thighs, cut into ½-inch pieces

2 cups chopped onion (about 2 medium)

3 garlic cloves, chopped

1 cup fresh corn kernels (about 2 ears) or frozen whole-kernel corn

1 cup water

1 tablespoon chopped jalapeño pepper

1 tablespoon chili powder

1½ teaspoons ground cumin

½ teaspoon salt

2 (14.5-ounce) cans no salt–added tomatoes, undrained and chopped

2 (14-ounce) cans fat-free, less-sodium chicken broth

1 (4.5-ounce) can chopped green chiles

2 (6-inch) corn tortillas, each cut into 8 wedges

5 tablespoons reduced-fat sour cream

Cilantro sprigs (optional)

1. Heat olive oil in a large Dutch oven over medium-high heat. Add chicken pieces and chopped onion, and cook 7 minutes or until onion is tender. Add chopped garlic to pan, and sauté 30 seconds. Stir in corn and next 8 ingredients. Bring to a boil, reduce heat, and simmer 45 minutes.
2. Preheat oven to 350°.
3. Place tortilla wedges on a baking sheet, and bake at 350° for 5 minutes or until crisp.
4. Ladle soup into individual bowls, and top with sour cream. Garnish with tortilla chips and, if desired, cilantro sprigs.

CALORIES 331; FAT 9.9g (sat 2.8g, mono 3.6g, poly 1.4g); PROTEIN 30.6g; CARB 30.9g; FIBER 6.1g; CHOL 77mg; IRON 2.3mg; SODIUM 983mg; CALC 130mg

Posole

Posole (poh-SOH-leh) is a thick, hearty soup from the Pacific Coast region of Mexico. It features chicken broth, fluffy white hominy, chopped onions, zesty jalapeño peppers, and vibrant green cilantro. It's traditionally served as a main course during the Christmas season. A lime garnish adds color and a festive look to your presentation.

Yield: 8 servings (serving size: 1½ cups soup, 1 tablespoon cilantro, 1½ teaspoons sour cream, and 1 lime wedge)

1 pound tomatillos

6 cups Brown Chicken Stock (recipe on facing page)

2 cups chopped onion

3 pounds chicken breast halves, skinned

4 garlic cloves, chopped

2 jalapeño peppers, seeded and quartered

1 (30-ounce) can white hominy, drained

1 teaspoon salt

½ cup chopped fresh cilantro

¼ cup reduced-fat sour cream

8 lime wedges

1. Discard husks and stems from the tomatillos. Cook whole tomatillos in boiling water 10 minutes or until tender; drain. Place tomatillos in a blender; process until smooth; set aside.

2. Place stock and next 5 ingredients in a large stockpot; bring to a boil. Cover, reduce heat, and simmer 35 minutes or until chicken is done. Remove chicken from bones; shred. Stir in pureed tomatillos and salt; cook 5 minutes or until heated. Stir in chicken, and serve with cilantro, sour cream, and lime wedges.

CALORIES 233; FAT 4.1g (sat 1.3g, mono 0.7g, poly 0.8g); PROTEIN 31.8g; CARB 19.4g; FIBER 4g; CHOL 79mg; IRON 1.8mg; SODIUM 548mg; CALC 46mg

INGREDIENT TIP

Tomatillos, a close cousin to tomatoes, have a tart flavor that make Mexican green sauces so distinct. They are about the size of a large cherry tomato, and they have a papery outer skin and a white inside that is meatier than a tomato.

Brown Chicken Stock

Use a pan large enough to roast the chicken and all the vegetables in a single layer. If the pan is too small, the chicken won't brown properly.

Yield: 10 cups (serving size: 1 cup)

¼ pound fennel stalks, cut into 2-inch-thick pieces

3 carrots, cut into 2-inch-thick pieces

1 celery stalk, cut into 2-inch-thick pieces

1 medium onion, unpeeled and quartered

6 pounds chicken pieces

½ teaspoon black peppercorns

6 fresh parsley sprigs

5 fresh thyme sprigs

2 bay leaves

16 cups cold water, divided

1. Preheat oven to 400°.

2. Arrange first 4 ingredients in the bottom of a broiler or roasting pan, and top with chicken pieces. Bake at 400° for 1½ hours, turning chicken once every 30 minutes (chicken and vegetables should be very brown).

3. Place peppercorns, parsley, thyme, and bay leaves in an 8-quart stockpot. Remove vegetables and chicken from broiler pan, and place in stockpot. Carefully discard drippings from broiler pan, leaving browned bits. Place broiler pan on stovetop, and add 4 cups water. Bring to a boil over medium-high heat. Reduce heat; simmer 10 minutes, scraping bottom to loosen browned bits.

4. Pour contents of broiler pan into stockpot. Add remaining 12 cups water, and bring to a boil over medium-high heat. Reduce heat; simmer 1½ hours.

5. Strain stock through a fine sieve into a large bowl. Reserve chicken for another use; discard remaining solids. Cover and chill stock 8 hours. Skim solidified fat from surface of broth, and discard.

CALORIES 31; FAT 1.1g (sat 0.3g, mono 0.4g, poly 0.2g); PROTEIN 4.7g; CARB 0.4g; FIBER 0.1g; CHOL 15mg; IRON 0.3mg; SODIUM 19mg; CALC 4mg

Coconut-Curry Chicken Soup

Start with shredded cooked chicken breast and transform your dinner tonight into restaurant-quality Thai cuisine. The coconut milk gives the soup a creamy, smooth texture.

Yield: 7 servings (serving size: 2 cups soup and 1 lime wedge)

4 cups water

3 cups fresh spinach leaves

½ pound snow peas, trimmed and cut in half crosswise

1 (5¾-ounce) package pad thai noodles (wide rice stick noodles)

1 tablespoon canola oil

¼ cup thinly sliced shallots

2 teaspoons red curry paste

1½ teaspoons curry powder

½ teaspoon ground turmeric

½ teaspoon ground coriander

2 garlic cloves, minced

6 cups fat-free, less-sodium chicken broth

1 (13.5-ounce) can light coconut milk

2½ cups shredded cooked chicken breast (about 1 pound)

½ cup chopped green onions

2 tablespoons sugar

2 tablespoons fish sauce

½ cup chopped fresh cilantro

4 small hot red chiles, seeded and chopped, or ¼ teaspoon crushed red pepper

7 lime wedges

1. Bring 4 cups water to a boil in a large saucepan. Add spinach and peas to pan; cook 30 seconds. Remove vegetables from pan with a slotted spoon; place in a large bowl. Add noodles to pan; cook 3 minutes. Drain; add noodles to spinach mixture in bowl.

2. Heat oil in pan over medium-high heat. Add shallots and next 5 ingredients to pan; sauté 1 minute. Add broth to pan; bring to a boil. Add coconut milk to pan; reduce heat, and simmer 5 minutes. Add chicken, onions, sugar, and fish sauce to pan; cook 2 minutes. Pour chicken mixture over noodle mixture in bowl. Stir in cilantro and chiles. Serve with lime wedges.

CALORIES 315; FAT 7.8g (sat 3.7g, mono 2.2g, poly 1.3g); PROTEIN 29.3g; CARB 30.9g; FIBER 2.4g; CHOL 62mg; IRON 3.2mg; SODIUM 841mg; CALC 78mg

Sweet and Spicy Chicken and White Bean Stew

Lemongrass lends a hint of citrus to this stew. Garnish with a cilantro sprig for that extra special touch.

Yield: 4 servings (serving size: 1¾ cups stew and 1 tablespoon cilantro)

2 tablespoons canola oil

½ teaspoon ground cardamom

⅛ teaspoon ground cloves

3 garlic cloves, minced

2 cups finely chopped onion

½ teaspoon chili powder

¼ teaspoon ground turmeric

½ teaspoon ground coriander

1 (15.5-ounce) can cannellini beans or other white beans, undrained

¾ pound skinless, boneless chicken breast, cut into bite-sized pieces

1 cup light coconut milk

½ cup water

1 tablespoon chopped peeled fresh lemongrass (about 1 stalk)

1 (14.5-ounce) can fire-roasted diced tomatoes, undrained

1 (8-ounce) baking potato, cut into ½-inch cubes

¼ cup chopped fresh cilantro

1. Heat oil in a Dutch oven over medium-high heat. Add cardamom, cloves, and garlic to pan; cook 30 seconds, stirring constantly. Add onion; sauté 8 minutes or until tender. Add chili powder, turmeric, and coriander; cook 30 seconds. Add beans and chicken; stir to coat. Add milk, ½ cup water, lemongrass, tomatoes, and potato to pan. Cover, reduce heat, and simmer 30 minutes or until potato is tender. Sprinkle each serving with cilantro.

CALORIES 364; FAT 11.7g (sat 3.7g, mono 4.4g, poly 2.8g); PROTEIN 27.3g; CARB 37.5g; FIBER 6.7g; CHOL 49mg; IRON 3.8mg; SODIUM 544mg; CALC 82mg

WINE TIP

With its layered spices and distinctly Asian ingredients, this chicken and bean stew finds its match in an off-dry riesling.

Brunswick Stew

From 19th-century Virginia, this stew originally included squirrel meat (we opt here for chicken). Although the stew is sometimes thickened with stale bread cubes, this version uses flour to give it body and features garlic bread on the side. Garnish with fresh thyme sprigs.

Yield: 6 servings (serving size: 1 cup stew and 1 slice bread)

Cooking spray

1 cup chopped red bell pepper

¾ cup chopped yellow onion

½ cup chopped celery

1 tablespoon peanut oil

1 tablespoon all-purpose flour

1 pound skinless, boneless chicken thighs, cut into ½-inch pieces

2 cups fat-free, less-sodium chicken broth

2 tablespoons no-salt-added tomato paste

1 teaspoon dried thyme

½ teaspoon salt

½ teaspoon hot pepper sauce (such as Tabasco)

1 (10-ounce) package frozen whole-kernel corn, thawed

1 (10-ounce) package frozen baby lima beans, thawed

6 (1-ounce) slices Italian bread, toasted

2 garlic cloves, halved

1. Heat a large Dutch oven over medium-high heat. Coat pan with cooking spray. Add bell pepper, onion, and celery to pan; cook 5 minutes, stirring occasionally. Add oil to pan. Combine flour and chicken in a medium bowl, tossing to coat. Add chicken to pan; cook 2 minutes or until lightly browned. Gradually stir in broth; bring to a boil. Cook 1 minute or until slightly thick, stirring constantly. Add tomato paste and next 5 ingredients to pan. Cover, reduce heat, and simmer 30 minutes.

2. Rub bread slices with cut sides of garlic; discard garlic. Serve bread with stew.

CALORIES 319; FAT 9.2g (sat 2.2g, mono 3.5g, poly 2.6g); PROTEIN 22.4g; CARB 38g; FIBER 5.8g; CHOL 50mg; IRON 3.2mg; SODIUM 596mg; CALC 58mg

Jamaican Chicken Stew

This classic Jamaican stew will usher you to the island in spirit and have you saying "Yah mon!" before your second bite. Add jalapeño-style corn bread and pineapple sorbet for a simple weeknight supper.

Yield: 4 servings (serving size: 1½ cups stew and ¾ cup rice)

1 cup uncooked long-grain rice

2 teaspoons olive oil

1 cup chopped onion

1 large garlic clove, minced

1 pound skinless, boneless chicken breast, cut into bite-sized pieces

1 teaspoon curry powder

1 teaspoon dried thyme

½ teaspoon ground allspice

½ teaspoon crushed red pepper

½ teaspoon cracked black pepper

¼ cup dry red wine

2 tablespoons capers

1 (15-ounce) can black beans, rinsed and drained

1 (14.5-ounce) can diced tomatoes, undrained

Cilantro sprigs (optional)

1. Prepare rice according to package directions, omitting salt and fat. Keep warm.

2. Heat oil in a large nonstick skillet over medium-high heat. Add onion and garlic; sauté 3 minutes or until tender. Combine chicken and next 5 ingredients. Add chicken mixture to pan; sauté 4 minutes. Stir in wine, capers, beans, and tomatoes. Cover, reduce heat, and simmer 10 minutes or until tender. Spoon rice into individual bowls; ladle stew over rice. Garnish with cilantro sprigs, if desired.

CALORIES 465; FAT 5g (sat 1g, mono 2.2g, poly 1g); PROTEIN 38.5g; CARB 66g; FIBER 5.9g; CHOL 66mg; IRON 6mg; SODIUM 799mg; CALC 101mg

INGREDIENT TIP

Canned beans are more convenient than dried beans. For the best results, rinse thoroughly  *with tap water before using, and drain in a colander. Rinsing canned beans gets rid of the thick liquid in the can and reduces the sodium by 40 percent.*

Dijon Chicken Stew with Potatoes and Kale

Here's a comforting and warming stew that's ideal to savor after a cold day of hiking or outdoor fun. Substitute Swiss chard or mustard greens for kale, if you prefer.

Yield: 6 servings (serving size: 1½ cups)

4 teaspoons olive oil, divided

2 cups sliced leek

4 garlic cloves, minced

1.5 ounces all-purpose flour (about ⅓ cup)

1 pound skinless, boneless chicken thighs, cut into bite-sized pieces

½ pound skinless, boneless chicken breast, cut into bite-sized pieces

½ teaspoon salt, divided

½ teaspoon freshly ground black pepper, divided

1 cup dry white wine

3 cups fat-free, less-sodium chicken broth, divided

1 tablespoon all-purpose flour

1½ cups water

2 tablespoons Dijon mustard

2 cups (½-inch) cubed peeled white potato (about 1 pound)

8 cups loosely packed torn kale (about 5 ounces)

Crushed red pepper (optional)

1. Heat 1 teaspoon oil in a Dutch oven over medium-high heat. Add sliced leek to pan, and sauté 6 minutes or until tender and golden brown. Add garlic; sauté 1 minute. Spoon leek mixture into a large bowl.

2. Place ⅓ cup flour in a shallow bowl or pie plate. Dredge chicken in flour, shaking off excess. Heat remaining 1 tablespoon oil in pan over medium-high heat. Add half of chicken mixture; sprinkle with ⅛ teaspoon salt and ⅛ teaspoon black pepper. Cook 6 minutes, browning on all sides. Add browned chicken to leek mixture. Repeat procedure with remaining chicken mixture, ⅛ teaspoon salt, and ⅛ teaspoon black pepper.

3. Add wine to pan, scraping pan to loosen browned bits. Combine 1 cup broth and 1 tablespoon flour, stirring with a whisk until smooth. Add broth mixture, remaining 2 cups broth, 1½ cups water, and mustard to pan; bring to a boil. Stir in chicken mixture, remaining ¼ teaspoon salt, and remaining ¼ teaspoon black pepper. Cover, reduce heat, and simmer 30 minutes.

4. Stir in potato. Cover and simmer 30 minutes or until potato is tender. Stir in kale; cover and simmer 10 minutes. Garnish with crushed red pepper, if desired.

CALORIES 324; FAT 7.9g (sat 1.5g, mono 3.5g, poly 1.7g); PROTEIN 30.9g; CARB 33.7g; FIBER 5g; CHOL 85mg; IRON 4.6mg; SODIUM 659mg; CALC 180mg

White Chili

This dish uses hot pepper sauce made from jalapeños; it's milder than the red hot pepper varieties. Stirring frequently toward the end of cooking time prevents the bean-thickened broth from sticking to the bottom and scorching. Serve with jalapeño corn bread.

Yield: 6 servings (serving size: about ¾ cup chili, 4 teaspoons yogurt, and 1 teaspoon green onions)

2 teaspoons canola oil

1½ cups chopped onion (about 1 large)

3 garlic cloves, minced

2 cups fat-free, less-sodium chicken broth

5 teaspoons green hot pepper sauce (such as Tabasco)

½ teaspoon kosher salt

1¼ pounds skinless, boneless chicken breast halves

2 tablespoons stone-ground cornmeal

1 (19-ounce) can cannellini beans or other white beans, rinsed and drained

½ cup plain fat-free yogurt

2 tablespoons thinly sliced green onions (about 1)

Lime wedges (optional)

1. Heat oil in a Dutch oven over medium heat. Add chopped onion and garlic to pan; cook 5 minutes or until onion is tender, stirring occasionally. Add broth, hot pepper sauce, salt, and chicken to pan; bring to a boil. Cover, reduce heat to low, and simmer 15 minutes. Remove chicken from broth mixture; cool.

2. Add cornmeal and beans to broth mixture, stirring with a whisk; simmer 15 minutes. Mash about ¼ cup beans against side of pan. Cut chicken into bite-sized pieces. Add chicken to pan; simmer 5 minutes or until mixture thickens, stirring frequently. Top each serving with yogurt; sprinkle with green onions. Serve with lime wedges, if desired.

CALORIES 198; FAT 4.1g (sat 0.8g, mono 1.7g, poly 1.2g); PROTEIN 24.8g; CARB 14.3g; FIBER 3g; CHOL 56mg; IRON 1.6mg; SODIUM 456mg; CALC 63mg

Chicken Chili with Pesto

Swirl in a generous dollop of pesto before serving to liven up this classic white chili.

Yield: 4 servings (serving size: 1¼ cups)

2 teaspoons vegetable oil

¾ cup finely chopped onion

¾ pound skinless, boneless chicken breast, cut into bite-sized pieces

1½ cups finely chopped carrot

¾ cup finely chopped red bell pepper

¾ cup thinly sliced celery

¼ cup canned chopped green chiles

¾ teaspoon dried oregano

½ teaspoon ground cumin

¼ teaspoon salt

⅛ teaspoon black pepper

1 (16-ounce) can cannellini beans or other white beans, rinsed and drained

1 (14½-ounce) can fat-free, less-sodium chicken broth

3 tablespoons Classic Pesto

1. Heat oil in a Dutch oven over medium-high heat. Add onion and chicken; sauté 5 minutes. Add carrot, bell pepper, and celery; sauté 4 minutes. Add chiles and next 6 ingredients; bring to a boil.

2. Cover, reduce heat, and simmer 25 minutes. Stir in Classic Pesto.

Note: The chili and pesto can be made ahead and frozen for up to 3 months. Prepare and freeze 3 tablespoons Classic Pesto. Prepare the chili without Classic Pesto, and spoon into a freezer-safe container. Cool completely in refrigerator; cover and freeze. Thaw chili and pesto in refrigerator. Place chili in a large skillet; cook over medium-low heat until thoroughly heated, stirring occasionally. Stir in Classic Pesto.

CALORIES 327; FAT 8.5g (sat 1.8g, mono 3.4g, poly 2.5g); PROTEIN 30.3g; CARB 30.7g; FIBER 5.9g; CHOL 52mg; IRON 4.1mg; SODIUM 769mg; CALC 134mg

Classic Pesto

Yield: ¾ cup (serving size: 1 tablespoon)

2 tablespoons coarsely chopped walnuts or pine nuts

2 garlic cloves, peeled

3 tablespoons extra-virgin olive oil

4 cups fresh basil leaves (about 4 ounces)

½ cup (2 ounces) grated fresh Parmesan cheese

¼ teaspoon salt

1. Drop nuts and garlic through food chute with food processor on; process until minced. Add oil; pulse 3 times. Add basil, cheese, and salt; process until finely minced, scraping sides of bowl once.

CALORIES 58; FAT 5.3g (sat 1.3g, mono 3g, poly 0.8g); PROTEIN 2.1g; CARB 0.9g; FIBER 0.6g; CHOL 3mg; IRON 0.5mg; SODIUM 125mg; CALC 72mg

Chicken Chowder with Chipotle

This hearty soup makes enough to feed a crowd and is simple to prepare on a weeknight.

Yield: 8 servings (serving size: about 1⅓ cups soup and 1 lime wedge)

1 (7-ounce) can chipotle chiles in adobo sauce

1 tablespoon extra-virgin olive oil

2 cups chopped onion

1 cup chopped carrot

½ cup chopped celery

1 teaspoon ground cumin

½ teaspoon dried oregano

½ teaspoon dried thyme

6 garlic cloves, crushed

6 cups fat-free, less-sodium chicken broth

1½ pounds skinless, boneless chicken breast

2 medium red potatoes (about 12 ounces), cut into ½-inch pieces

1 (15.5-ounce) can white or golden hominy, rinsed and drained

¼ cup whipping cream

1 cup chopped seeded plum tomato

¼ cup chopped fresh cilantro

½ teaspoon salt

8 lime wedges

1. Remove 1 chile and 1 teaspoon adobo sauce from can; reserve remaining chiles and sauce for another use. Finely chop chile; set chile and sauce aside separately.

2. Heat oil in a large Dutch oven over medium heat. Add chopped chile, onion, and next 6 ingredients; cook 7 minutes or until onion is tender, stirring frequently. Stir in broth; bring to a boil. Add chicken; cover, reduce heat to medium-low, and simmer 30 minutes or until chicken is tender. Remove chicken with a slotted spoon, and cool slightly. Shred chicken with 2 forks; cover and keep warm.

3. Remove pan from heat; let stand 5 minutes. Place one-third of broth mixture in a blender; process until smooth. Pour pureed broth mixture into a large bowl. Repeat procedure in two more batches with remaining broth mixture. Return pureed broth mixture to pan. Stir in potatoes and hominy; bring to a simmer over medium heat. Cook, uncovered, 20 minutes or until potatoes are tender. Stir in chicken and cream; simmer 5 minutes. Remove from heat, and stir in reserved adobo sauce, tomato, cilantro, and salt. Serve with lime wedges.

CALORIES 246; FAT 6.2g (sat 2.3g, mono 2.4g, poly 0.8g); PROTEIN 24.5g; CARB 21.8g; FIBER 3.5g; CHOL 60mg; IRON 1.7mg; SODIUM 672mg; CALC 52mg

Chicken Corn Chowder

Corn kernels pureed with milk create the rich, smooth texture of classic chowder. A tossed salad rounds out the meal.

Yield: 4 servings

1 tablespoon butter

6 green onions

2 tablespoons all-purpose flour

2 cups chopped cooked chicken breast

¼ teaspoon salt

¼ teaspoon freshly ground black pepper

2 (10-ounce) packages frozen corn kernels, thawed and divided

1 (14-ounce) can fat-free, less-sodium chicken broth

2 cups fat-free milk

½ cup (2 ounces) preshredded cheddar cheese

1. Melt butter in a Dutch oven over medium-high heat. Remove green tops from green onions. Chop green onion tops; set aside. Thinly slice white portion of each onion. Add sliced onions to pan; sauté 2 minutes. Add flour; cook 1 minute, stirring constantly with a whisk. Stir in chicken, salt, pepper, 1 package of corn, and broth; bring to a boil. Reduce heat, and simmer 5 minutes.

2. While mixture simmers, place remaining corn and milk in a blender; process until smooth. Add milk mixture to pan; simmer 2 minutes or until thoroughly heated. Ladle 2 cups chowder into each of 4 soup bowls; sprinkle evenly with green onion tops. Top each serving with 2 tablespoons cheese.

CALORIES 394; FAT 11.5g (sat 5.8g, mono 3.4g, poly 1.4g); PROTEIN 35.5g; CARB 40.7g; FIBER 4.5g; CHOL 84mg; IRON 2.2mg; SODIUM 534mg; CALC 293mg

Sausage and Chicken Gumbo

The quick versatility of frozen vegetables speeds up this recipe, making it ideal for weeknight fare. It hits the spot on a cool autumn evening.

Yield: 4 servings (serving size: 1½ cups gumbo and ½ cup rice)

1 (3½-ounce) bag boil-in-bag rice

2 tablespoons all-purpose flour

1 tablespoon vegetable oil

1 cup frozen chopped onion

1 cup frozen chopped green bell pepper

1 cup frozen cut okra

1 cup chopped celery

1 teaspoon bottled minced garlic

½ teaspoon dried thyme

¼ teaspoon ground red pepper

2 cups chopped roasted skinless, boneless chicken breast (about 2 breasts)

8 ounces turkey kielbasa, cut into 1-inch pieces

1 (14½-ounce) can diced tomatoes with peppers and onion

1 (14½-ounce) can fat-free, less-sodium chicken broth

1. Cook rice according to package directions, omitting salt and fat.

2. While rice cooks, combine flour and oil in a Dutch oven; sauté over medium-high heat 3 minutes. Add onion and next 6 ingredients, and cook 3 minutes or until tender, stirring frequently.

3. Stir in chicken, kielbasa, tomatoes, and broth; cook 6 minutes or until thoroughly heated. Serve over rice.

CALORIES 369; FAT 11.3g (sat 2.7g, mono 4.8g, poly 3g); PROTEIN 29.4g; CARB 37g; FIBER 3g; CHOL 77mg; IRON 2.2mg; SODIUM 949mg; CALC 92mg

simple side dishes

Sautéed Apples

Easy and simple, these apples are just perfect—you won't want to change a thing. They make a delicious accompaniment to not only chicken, but pork and just about any other main dish, too.

Yield: 8 servings (serving size: ½ cup)

3 tablespoons butter or margarine

6 cups sliced peeled Granny Smith apple (about 2 pounds)

½ cup packed brown sugar

⅛ teaspoon ground cinnamon

1. Melt butter in a large skillet over medium-high heat. Add apple; sauté 6 minutes or until apple is just tender. Stir in sugar and cinnamon. Cook 1 minute or until sugar melts.

CALORIES 137; FAT 4.6g (sat 2.7g, mono 1.3g, poly 0.2g); PROTEIN 0.2g; CARB 25.7g; FIBER 1.6g; CHOL 12mg; IRON 0.3mg; SODIUM 49mg; CALC 17mg

INGREDIENT TIP

Granny Smith apples are our hands-down favorite when it comes to cooking apples.

They remain tart, juicy, and crispy. They are simply a natural choice. Braeburns, however, make a good substitute.

Grilled Asparagus with Balsamic Vinegar

If you're looking for a change of pace from plain old steamed asparagus, here's a refreshing option. It's easy, quick, and flavorful.

Yield: 4 servings

1 pound thin asparagus spears

1 teaspoon olive oil

¼ teaspoon kosher salt

⅛ teaspoon freshly ground black pepper

Cooking spray

1 tablespoon balsamic vinegar

1. Prepare grill.

2. Snap off tough ends of asparagus, and place in a bowl or shallow dish. Drizzle asparagus with oil; sprinkle with salt and pepper, tossing well to coat. Place asparagus on a grill rack coated with cooking spray; grill 2 minutes on each side or until crisp-tender. Place asparagus in a bowl; drizzle with vinegar. Serve immediately.

CALORIES 25; FAT 1.2g (sat 0.2g, mono 0.8g, poly 0.2g); PROTEIN 1.3g; CARB 3g; FIBER 0g; CHOL 0mg; IRON 1.3mg; SODIUM 120mg; CALC 16mg

FLAVOR TIP

Some traditionally produced balsamic vinegars are aged for decades. They're quite expensive but definitely worth the splurge.

Chive Green Beans

Leave green beans whole for a restaurant-style look. Try this recipe with other vegetables, such as steamed carrots or fresh asparagus.

Yield: 4 servings (serving size: ¾ cup)

1 pound fresh green beans, trimmed

1 tablespoon chopped fresh chives

1 tablespoon chopped fresh parsley

2 teaspoons butter

½ teaspoon stone-ground mustard

¼ teaspoon salt

⅛ teaspoon pepper

1. Steam green beans, covered, 5 minutes or until crisp-tender. Remove from steamer; toss with remaining ingredients.

CALORIES 53; FAT 1.9g (sat 1.2g, mono 0.6g, poly 0.1g); PROTEIN 1.5g; CARB 7.1g; FIBER 4.2g; CHOL 5mg; IRON 0.6mg; SODIUM 175mg; CALC 58mg

NUTRITION TIP

Steaming helps vegetables retain their water-soluble vitamins, unlike boiling, which surrounds food with water causing the nutrients to leach out. More nutrients remain inside steamed vegetables because little water is used and there is minimal contact between the food and water.

Simple Garlicky Lima Beans

This is a delicious, basic way to cook any kind of fresh shell bean or pea. You can add these cooked beans to salads. For another variation, drizzle with olive oil and lemon juice, and sprinkle with crushed red pepper or a few shavings of Parmesan cheese.

Yield: 8 servings (serving size: ½ cup)

4 cups fresh lima beans

2½ cups water

1 tablespoon olive oil

2 garlic cloves, crushed

3 fresh thyme sprigs

1 bay leaf

½ teaspoon sea salt

¼ teaspoon freshly ground black pepper

1. Sort and wash beans; drain. Combine beans and next 5 ingredients in a medium saucepan. Bring to a boil. Cover, reduce heat, and simmer 20 minutes or until tender. Discard thyme sprigs and bay leaf. Stir in salt and pepper.

CALORIES 105; FAT 2.4g (sat 0.4g, mono 1.3g, poly 0.5g); PROTEIN 5.4g; CARB 16.2g; FIBER 3.9g; CHOL 0mg; IRON 2.5mg; SODIUM 152mg; CALC 30mg

Broccoli with Red Pepper Flakes and Toasted Garlic

The bold, straightforward flavors of garlic and crushed red pepper make this classic Mediterranean broccoli dish especially appealing.

Yield: 4 servings (serving size: 1 cup)

2 teaspoons olive oil

6 cups broccoli florets (about 1 head)

¼ teaspoon kosher salt

¼ teaspoon crushed red pepper

3 garlic cloves, thinly sliced

¼ cup water

1. Heat olive oil in a large nonstick skillet over medium-high heat. Add broccoli, kosher salt, crushed red pepper, and sliced garlic. Sauté 2 minutes. Add ¼ cup water. Cover, reduce heat to low, and cook 2 minutes or until broccoli is crisp-tender.

CALORIES 53; FAT 2.7g (sat 0.4g, mono 1.7g, poly 0.4g); PROTEIN 3.3g; CARB 6.4g; FIBER 3.2g; CHOL 0mg; IRON 1mg; SODIUM 147mg; CALC 55mg

INGREDIENT TIP

For chefs and many home cooks, Kosher salt, a cousin of table salt, has become the standard. Kosher salt, named as such because it's used by Jewish butchers, is chemically identical to table salt. But it has fewer additives and comes in coarser particles, which makes it easy to pinch and sprinkle.

Steamed Brussels Sprouts and Cauliflower with Walnuts

This quick and versatile side dish is good with beef and pork roasts or chicken. A serving boasts nearly one-fourth of daily fiber needs while the walnuts add a dose of heart-healthy unsaturated fat.

Yield: 6 servings (serving size: about ¾ cup)

6 tablespoons coarsely chopped walnuts

2¼ cups trimmed Brussels sprouts (about 1 pound), halved

3 cups cauliflower florets

½ teaspoon kosher salt

¼ teaspoon freshly ground black pepper

½ teaspoon fresh lemon juice

1. Place walnuts in a small skillet over medium heat; cook 3 minutes or until walnuts are lightly browned, shaking pan frequently. Remove from heat.
2. Steam Brussels sprouts, covered, 10 minutes or until tender. Add cauliflower to pan; steam, covered, 2 minutes or just until tender. Drain. Combine Brussels sprouts, cauliflower, salt, pepper, and juice in a medium bowl; toss to combine. Sprinkle evenly with walnuts.

CALORIES 104; FAT 3.5g (sat 0.4g, mono 0.5g, poly 2.5g); PROTEIN 6.4g; CARB 15.2g; FIBER 6.3g; CHOL 0mg; IRON 1.8mg; SODIUM 222mg; CALC 68mg

FLAVOR TIP

Toasting the walnuts heightens their flavor, much like meat is flavored by browning. It intensifies their nuttiness so you can use just a few nuts and still get big flavor.

Spiced Braised Carrots with Olives and Mint

Trust us—we know carrots! This unique recipe features an unlikely combination of ingredients—carrots, olives, and mint. Pair with grilled chicken to round out your meal.

Yield: 5 servings (serving size: about 1 cup)

2 cups water

5 cups (1-inch) slices carrots (about 2 pounds)

1½ tablespoons honey

1 tablespoon fresh lemon juice

½ teaspoon sea salt

½ teaspoon coriander seeds

¼ teaspoon crushed red pepper

1 (5-inch) fresh mint sprig

1 (2-inch) cinnamon stick

1 garlic clove, minced

¼ cup oil-cured black olives, pitted and coarsely chopped

1 teaspoon rice vinegar

1 teaspoon extra-virgin olive oil

1 teaspoon chopped fresh mint

Mint sprigs (optional)

1. Bring 2 cups water to a simmer in a large saucepan. Stir in carrots and next 8 ingredients; cover and simmer 15 minutes or until carrots are tender. Remove carrots with a slotted spoon, reserving liquid.

2. Bring liquid to a boil; cook until reduced to ¼ cup (about 10 minutes). Discard mint sprig and cinnamon stick. Return carrots to pan; stir in olives, vinegar, and oil. Cook 1 minute or until heated. Sprinkle with chopped mint. Garnish with mint sprigs, if desired.

CALORIES 139; FAT 4.1g (sat 0.5g, mono 2.8g, poly 0.5g); PROTEIN 2.2g; CARB 25.7g; FIBER 5.7g; CHOL 0mg; IRON 1.1mg; SODIUM 470mg; CALC 57mg

Two-Step Macaroni and Cheese

Processed cheese is a must in this quintessential quick-and-easy dish. It melts easily and gets smooth and creamy without help from flour, eggs, or other ingredients used in fancier counterparts. You can make prep even simpler by heating the first four ingredients in the microwave for about 3 minutes in a covered dish instead of cooking them on the stovetop.

Yield: 4 servings (serving size: ½ cup)

½ cup 1% low-fat milk

¼ teaspoon dry mustard

¼ teaspoon black pepper

6 ounces processed cheese (such as Velveeta), cubed

4 cups hot cooked elbow macaroni (about 8 ounces uncooked pasta)

1. Combine first 4 ingredients in a large saucepan over medium heat, stirring frequently; cook until smooth. Remove from heat; stir in macaroni. Serve immediately.

CALORIES 327; FAT 10.3g (sat 5.5g, mono 2.9g, poly 0.6g); PROTEIN 14.8g; CARB 43g; FIBER 2.2g; CHOL 29mg; IRON 2mg; SODIUM 659mg; CALC 277mg

INGREDIENT TIP

Processed cheese retains the flavor of natural cheese, but it has a longer storage life and melts smoothly to create a velvety texture.

Basic Pot of Peas

Although this recipe calls for pink-eyed peas, you can use black-eyed peas or other local varieties, too.

Yield: 6 servings (serving size: ½ cup)

2 teaspoons olive oil

½ cup chopped onion

2 garlic cloves, minced

3 cups fresh pink-eyed peas

3 cups water

3 bacon slices

½ teaspoon salt

½ teaspoon black pepper

1. Heat oil in a large saucepan over medium-high heat. Add onion and garlic; sauté 2 minutes. Add peas, water, and bacon; bring to a boil. Reduce heat; simmer, partially covered, 30 minutes or until tender. Discard bacon. Stir in salt and pepper.

CALORIES 167; FAT 5.3g (sat 1.6g, mono 2.8g, poly 0.6g); PROTEIN 4.1g; CARB 26.1g; FIBER 6.3g; CHOL 3mg; IRON 1.4mg; SODIUM 588mg; CALC 157mg

INGREDIENT TIP

Although most of the peas in this country are sold frozen, fresh ones are worth the search and the fingerwork. Choose young pods that are well filled and velvety soft to the touch. Peas that seem about to explode are too mature and will taste tough and mealy when cooked.

Buttermilk-Parmesan Mashed Potatoes

Pair these potatoes with chicken for comfort food at its finest.

Yield: 6 servings (serving size: ¾ cup)

2 pounds russet potatoes

⅔ cup fat-free milk

3 tablespoons butter

½ cup buttermilk

⅓ cup (1½ ounces) grated fresh Parmigiano-Reggiano cheese

½ teaspoon salt

¼ teaspoon freshly ground black pepper

1. Prick each potato several times with a fork. Place potatoes in the microwave, and cook at HIGH 16 minutes or until tender, turning after 8 minutes. Let stand 2 minutes. Cut each potato in half lengthwise; scoop out flesh with a large spoon, and transfer to a bowl.

2. Combine milk and butter in a microwave-safe bowl, and microwave at HIGH 2 minutes or until butter melts. Add milk mixture to potatoes; mash with a potato masher to desired consistency. Stir in buttermilk and remaining ingredients.

CALORIES 240; FAT 7.9g (sat 4.9g, mono 1.9g, poly 0.3g); PROTEIN 7.5g; CARB 35.2g; FIBER 3.5g; CHOL 22mg; IRON 1.7mg; SODIUM 366mg; CALC 117mg

FLAVOR TIP

Be sure to purchase a crumbly wedge of Parmigiano-Reggiano for this quick potato side dish. It gives these potatoes just the right amount of flavor without overpowering them.

Roasted Potatoes with Tangy Watercress Sauce

Add watercress, basil, and mint to a yogurt base for a fragrant, fresh-tasting sauce you can make up to two days ahead. Serve this versatile dish alongside chicken, beef, or lamb. You can also use the sauce as a dip for vegetables.

Yield: 8 servings (serving size: 1 cup potatoes and 2 tablespoons sauce)

Sauce:

1½ cups plain fat-free yogurt

1 cup trimmed watercress

⅓ cup light mayonnaise

¼ cup chopped green onions

3 tablespoons chopped fresh basil

1 tablespoon chopped fresh mint

1 teaspoon balsamic vinegar

¼ teaspoon salt

⅛ teaspoon freshly ground black pepper

Potatoes:

3 pounds small red potatoes, quartered

1½ tablespoons olive oil

1 teaspoon freshly ground black pepper

½ teaspoon salt

Cooking spray

1. Preheat oven to 450°.

2. To prepare sauce, place first 9 ingredients in a food processor or blender; process until smooth, scraping sides. Cover and chill.

3. To prepare potatoes, combine potatoes, oil, pepper, and salt in a jelly-roll pan or shallow roasting pan coated with cooking spray, tossing to coat. Bake at 450° for 35 minutes or until tender, stirring occasionally. Serve with sauce.

CALORIES 210; FAT 6.1g (sat 0.9g, mono 1.9g, poly 0.3g); PROTEIN 6.6g; CARB 33.2g; FIBER 3.1g; CHOL 4mg; IRON 2.6mg; SODIUM 347mg; CALC 123mg

INGREDIENT TIP

Watercress is a member of the mustard family. It has small, crisp dark green leaves with a sharp, peppery flavor. Pungent-flavored arugula makes a good substitute.

Poppy Seed Fruited Slaw

If you prefer slaws without mayo, you'll like this fruited variation. You can combine and refrigerate the dressing up to a day ahead. Serve with baked chicken, or take it to a picnic or backyard barbecue.

Yield: 6 servings (serving size: 1 cup)

Coleslaw:

½ cup orange sections

1 cup halved seedless red grapes

1 (16-ounce) package cabbage-and-carrot coleslaw

Dressing:

¼ cup sugar

1 tablespoon minced fresh onion

3 tablespoons cider vinegar

1 teaspoon poppy seeds

4 teaspoons canola oil

½ teaspoon dry mustard

¼ teaspoon salt

1. To prepare coleslaw, chop orange sections. Combine chopped oranges, grapes, and coleslaw in a large bowl.

2. To prepare dressing, combine ¼ cup sugar and remaining ingredients, stirring with a whisk until sugar dissolves. Add dressing mixture to cabbage mixture, and toss well. Cover and chill 30 minutes before serving.

CALORIES 114; FAT 3.6g (sat 0.3g, mono 1.9g, poly 1.1g); PROTEIN 1.6g; CARB 21.3g; FIBER 1g; CHOL 0mg; IRON 0.7mg; SODIUM 114mg; CALC 56mg

QUICK TIP

Once the rind and white pith have been removed from your orange, hold the fruit in your palm. Gently follow the natural sections of the orange with a knife to cut out wedges or sections.

Squash-Rice Casserole

Easy to prepare and rich in flavor, this casserole pairs fabulously with roasted chicken, ham, or pork chops. This simple dish has become a staff favorite, and we believe it will be right at home in your home, too.

Yield: 8 servings (serving size: 1 cup)

8 cups sliced zucchini (about 2½ pounds)

1 cup chopped onion

½ cup fat-free, less-sodium chicken broth

2 cups cooked rice

1 cup (4 ounces) shredded reduced-fat sharp cheddar cheese

1 cup fat-free sour cream

¼ cup (1 ounce) grated fresh Parmesan cheese, divided

¼ cup Italian-seasoned breadcrumbs

1 teaspoon salt

¼ teaspoon black pepper

2 large eggs, lightly beaten

Cooking spray

1. Preheat oven to 350°.

2. Combine first 3 ingredients in a Dutch oven; bring to a boil. Cover, reduce heat, and simmer 20 minutes or until tender. Drain; partially mash with a potato masher.

3. Combine zucchini mixture, rice, cheddar cheese, sour cream, 2 tablespoons Parmesan cheese, breadcrumbs, salt, pepper, and eggs in a bowl; stir gently. Spoon mixture into a 13 x 9–inch baking dish coated with cooking spray; sprinkle with 2 tablespoons Parmesan cheese. Bake at 350° for 30 minutes or until bubbly.

4. Preheat broiler. Broil 1 minute or until lightly browned.

CALORIES 197; FAT 5.5g (sat 2.7g, mono 1.5g, poly 0.4g); PROTEIN 12.7g; CARB 24g; FIBER 1.4g; CHOL 65mg; IRON 1.5mg; SODIUM 623mg; CALC 209mg

Charred Summer Vegetables

Serve with grilled pork, chicken, or fish. Add the vegetables to a hot cast-iron skillet, cover, and cook 5 minutes without stirring so the natural sugars caramelize and add flavor.

Yield: 6 servings (serving size: ⅔ cup)

Cooking spray

2½ cups fresh corn kernels (about 5 ears)

2 cups chopped green beans (about 8 ounces)

1 cup chopped zucchini (about 4 ounces)

1 cup chopped red bell pepper

2 tablespoons finely chopped shallots

1 tablespoon chopped fresh flat-leaf parsley

2 tablespoons fresh lemon juice

4 teaspoons extra-virgin olive oil

½ teaspoon salt

½ teaspoon chopped fresh thyme

¼ teaspoon freshly ground black pepper

1. Heat a 12-inch cast-iron skillet over high heat. Coat pan with cooking spray. Add corn kernels, chopped green beans, chopped zucchini, and chopped bell pepper to pan; stir to combine. Cover and cook 5 minutes. Combine shallots and remaining ingredients in a bowl, stirring well. Add shallot mixture to corn mixture; toss to coat.

CALORIES 102; FAT 3.2g (sat 0.3g, mono 1.7g, poly 0.3g); PROTEIN 3.3g; CARB 18.5g; FIBER 2.7g; CHOL 0mg; IRON 0.8mg; SODIUM 210mg; CALC 31mg

Nutritional Analysis

How to Use It and Why

Glance at the end of any *Cooking Light* recipe, and you'll see how committed we are to helping you make the best of today's light cooking. With chefs, registered dietitians, home economists, and a computer system that analyzes every ingredient we use, *Cooking Light* gives you authoritative dietary detail like no other magazine. We go to such lengths so you can see how our recipes fit into your healthful eating plan. If you're trying to lose weight, the calorie and fat figures will probably help most. But if you're keeping a close eye on the sodium, cholesterol, and saturated fat in your diet, we provide those numbers, too. And because many women don't get enough iron or calcium, we can also help there, as well. Finally, there's a fiber analysis for those of us who don't get enough roughage.

Here's a helpful guide to put our nutritional analysis numbers into perspective. Remember, one size doesn't fit all, so take your lifestyle, age, and circumstances into consideration when determining your nutrition needs. For example, pregnant or breast-feeding women need more protein, calories, and calcium. And men older than 50 need 1,200mg of calcium daily, 200mg more than the amount recommended for younger men.

In Our Nutritional Analysis, We Use These Abbreviations

sat	saturated fat	**CHOL**	cholesterol
mono	monounsaturated fat	**CALC**	calcium
poly	polyunsaturated fat	**g**	gram
CARB	carbohydrates	**mg**	milligram

Daily Nutrition Guide

	Women Ages 25 to 50	Women over 50	Men over 24
Calories	2,000	2,000 or less	2,700
Protein	50g	50g or less	63g
Fat	65g or less	65g or less	88g or less
Saturated Fat	20g or less	20g or less	27g or less
Carbohydrates	304g	304g	410g
Fiber	25g to 35g	25g to 35g	25g to 35g
Cholesterol	300mg or less	300mg or less	300mg or less
Iron	18mg	8mg	8mg
Sodium	2,300mg or less	1,500mg or less	2,300mg or less
Calcium	1,000mg	1,200mg	1,000mg

The nutritional values used in our calculations either come from The Food Processor, Version 8.9 (ESHA Research), or are provided by food manufacturers.

Metric Equivalents

The information in the following charts is provided to help cooks outside the United States successfully use the recipes in this book. All equivalents are approximate.

Cooking/Oven Temperatures

	Fahrenheit	Celsius	Gas Mark
Freeze Water	32° F	0° C	
Room Temp.	68° F	20° C	
Boil Water	212° F	100° C	
Bake	325° F	160° C	3
	350° F	180° C	4
	375° F	190° C	5
	400° F	200° C	6
	425° F	220° C	7
	450° F	230° C	8
Broil			Grill

Liquid Ingredients by Volume

¼ tsp	=					1 ml		
½ tsp	=					2 ml		
1 tsp	=					5 ml		
3 tsp	=	1 tbl	=	½ fl oz	=	15 ml		
2 tbls	=	⅛ cup	=	1 fl oz	=	30 ml		
4 tbls	=	¼ cup	=	2 fl oz	=	60 ml		
5⅓ tbls	=	⅓ cup	=	3 fl oz	=	80 ml		
8 tbls	=	½ cup	=	4 fl oz	=	120 ml		
10⅔ tbls	=	⅔ cup	=	5 fl oz	=	160 ml		
12 tbls	=	¾ cup	=	6 fl oz	=	180 ml		
16 tbls	=	1 cup	=	8 fl oz	=	240 ml		
1 pt	=	2 cups	=	16 fl oz	=	480 ml		
1 qt	=	4 cups	=	32 fl oz	=	960 ml		
				33 fl oz	=	1000 ml	=	1 l

Dry Ingredients by Weight

(To convert ounces to grams, multiply the number of ounces by 30.)

1 oz	=	¹⁄₁₆ lb	=	30 g
4 oz	=	¼ lb	=	120 g
8 oz	=	½ lb	=	240 g
12 oz	=	¾ lb	=	360 g
16 oz	=	1 lb	=	480 g

Length

(To convert inches to centimeters, multiply the number of inches by 2.5.)

1 in	=					2.5 cm		
6 in	=	½ ft			=	15 cm		
12 in	=	1 ft			=	30 cm		
36 in	=	3 ft	=	1 yd	=	90 cm		
40 in	=					100 cm	=	1 m

Equivalents for Different Types of Ingredients

Standard Cup	Fine Powder (ex. flour)	Grain (ex. rice)	Granular (ex. sugar)	Liquid Solids (ex. butter)	Liquid (ex. milk)
1	140 g	150 g	190 g	200 g	240 ml
¾	105 g	113 g	143 g	150 g	180 ml
⅔	93 g	100 g	125 g	133 g	160 ml
½	70 g	75 g	95 g	100 g	120 ml
⅓	47 g	50 g	63 g	67 g	80 ml
¼	35 g	38 g	48 g	50 g	60 ml
⅛	18 g	19 g	24 g	25 g	30 ml